S O C

C O N T R O L

T H R O U G H

L A W

SOCIAL CONTROL THROUGH LAW

ROSCOE POUND

WITH A NEW INTRODUCTION BY A. JAVIER TREVIÑO

Transaction Publishers
New Brunswick (U.S.A.) and London (U.K.)

New material this edition copyright © 1997 by Transaction Publishers, New Brunswick, New Jersey 08903. Originally published in 1942 by Yale University Press.

This book is printed on acid-free paper that meets the American National Standard for Permanence of Paper for Printed Library Materials.

Library of Congress Catalog Number: 96-2793
ISBN: 1-56000-916-0
Printed in the United States of America

Library of Congress Cataloging-in-Publication Data

Pound, Roscoe, 1870–1964.
Social control through law / Roscoe Pound ; with a new introduction by A. Javier Treviño.
p. cm.
Originally published: New Haven : Yale University Press, © 1942.
Includes index.
ISBN 1-56000-916-0 (pbk. : alk. paper)
1. Law—Philosophy. 2. Sociological jurisprudence. 3. Social control. I. Title.
K230.P67S66 1996
340'.115—dc20 96-2793
CIP

CONTENTS

THIS republication of Roscoe Pound's *Social Control Through Law* will no doubt be enthusiastically greeted by a new generation of jurists, legal theorists, and sociologists. Perhaps no other volume produced by Pound can, in one small package, better convey the whole of his thought. Many of the basic themes that Pound repeatedly expounds (albeit from different angles) in his numerous works are contained in this small book—the scope and subject matter of law, legal history and comparative law, the nature of law, law and morals, sociological jurisprudence, the jural postulates, the engineering theory, social control, and the survey of social interests. In *Social Control Through Law* we find Pound as a jurist, philosopher, and scientist. To be sure, Pound possessed extended erudition in many kinds of scholarship besides legal scholarship. His breadth of reading and inexhaustible learning induced Oliver Wendell Holmes to proclaim that it made him tired just to try to remember the titles of what Pound "knows." Pound surveyed the law so widely and thoroughly that, at the time of his death, the bibliography of his publications consisted of close to a thousand titles, of which several hundred were books and major essays, many of which were intended for a general audience. My intention in this introduction is to briefly outline the principal aspects of Roscoe Pound's legal philosophy, as it was conveyed in several books, articles, and addresses, and show their relation to *Social Control Through Law*.

I

The broad details of Pound's academic career are relatively well known. He was born on October 27, 1870, in the frontier town of Lincoln, Nebraska, the capital of the then newest state in the Union. His father, Stephen Bosworth Pound, was a successful lawyer and a district court judge. The young Roscoe was educated at home by his mother, Laura Biddlecomb Pound, until the time that he enrolled in Latin School. At the age of thirteen, Pound entered the University of Nebraska where he majored in botany, thus acquiring a thorough grounding in the method of the natural sciences. The importance that Pound gave to empirical investigation was to influence his approach to jurisprudence throughout his long and active career. Indeed, Pound had a penchant for collecting and systematically classifying and cataloging legal ideas much as a botanist would collect, classify, and catalogue various botanical species. This taxonomic approach is especially evident in Pound's *Outlines of Lectures on Jurisprudence* (1903) where he engages in the scientific ordering, the "botanization" as it were, of minutely detailed judicial terms.

Pound graduated from the University of Nebraska in 1888 and the following year received his M.A. degree in botany. Although hardly surprising, it is nevertheless interesting that despite Pound's love of botany, his initial fascination with law was sparked by his father. During Pound's junior year in college his father gave him three books on jurisprudence which Pound repeatedly read: Holland's *Elements of Jurisprudence,* Amos's *Science of Law,* and Maine's *Ancient Law*. These three volumes may well have inspired Pound to pursue legal study in earnest. But since the University of Nebraska did not, at that time, offer professional training in law, Pound went East in the fall of 1889 to attend Harvard Law

School. He spent only one year at Harvard, leaving the law school, as he put it, "a convinced utilitarian" and a follower of the nineteenth-century British legal philosopher John Austin. To be sure, Pound remained a social utilitarian throughout his life (even if his utilitarianism was continuously modified), but it was not long before he partially eschewed Austin's well-known proposal that the sanction of law is found in the threat of a sovereign. In contrast, for Pound the justification of law is found in the social ends that law, as an instrument of the community, must serve. Nevertheless, Pound seems to have retained Austin's idea that force is an essential element of law. As he states in *Social Control Through Law,* "it is well to remember that if law as a mode of social control has all the strength of force, it has also all the weaknesses of dependence on force" (p. 20). Pound, however, makes it clear that force is only a means, not an end in itself.

Aside from his intensive year at Harvard Pound never again undertook any other formal study of the law or completed the prescribed requirements for a law degree. The scantiness of his legal education notwithstand-

ing, he became one of the foremost legal scholars of all time. Some years after his Harvard
experience Pound implored law teachers, or
"legal monks" as he derisively called them, to
supplement the traditional subject-matter of
legal study to include a scientific understanding of the relations of law and society and of
the needs and interests of modern industrial
life.

Upon leaving Harvard Pound returned to
Lincoln, qualified for the Nebraska bar, and
began to apprentice at his father's law firm.
Busy starting his practice in Lincoln, Pound
initially wavered a bit between professions. In
1892 he founded and became director of the
Botanical Survey of Nebraska, an organization with a university affiliation, which helped
Pound launch his plan for the systematic botanical exploration of Nebraska. Five years
later he completed his dissertation, the *Phyto-
geography of Nebraska,* a landmark scientific
treatise on American plant ecology which
earned him a Ph.D. in botany. The requirements for the degree included a minor as well
as a major and Pound opted to minor in Roman Law. Shortly after graduating Pound re-
solved to embark on a legal career and started

out by writing briefs with his father and by arguing appeals in state and federal courts. In 1899 he was appointed an assistant professor of jurisprudence and international law at the University of Nebraska College of Law.

Although Pound spent over sixty years involved chiefly in the administrative and teaching tasks of academe, he periodically enjoyed brief sojourns in the active practice of law. One such interval occurred in 1901 when, at the age of thirty, Pound was named as one of nine commissioners (auxiliary judges) of appeals of the Supreme Court of Nebraska in a move to expedite an overflow of judicial cases. The commissioner's "recommendations" were not superficial and cursory rhetoric on particular cases; rather they were taken, pro forma, as the judicial decisions of the court. While serving as commissioner Pound prepared recommendations in more than 200 cases.

In 1903 Pound relinquished his judicial duties and returned to academe, becoming dean of the College of Law at Nebraska. Around this time his formulation of sociological jurisprudence took its initial and foundational form. Apparently attracted to Pound's "progressive" views, John H. Wigmore, dean of the Northwestern University School of Law appointed him professor of law in 1907. After only a short period at Northwestern, Pound accepted a professorship at the University of Chicago, and one year after that Dean Ezra Thayer brought him to Harvard as Story Professor of Law. In 1913 Pound was made Carter Professor of General Jurisprudence, a title that more closely reflected his dominant interest. While at Harvard he served as dean for twenty years before being given one of the newly instituted University Professorships in 1936. Though he formally became emeritus in 1947 at the age of seventy-seven, Pound continued to publish prolifically until his death in 1964.

In addition to these regular teaching positions, Pound held a variety of distinguished visiting lectureships at several universities including Yale, Dartmouth, Cambridge, Tulane, and North Carolina. Many of his lectures were subsequently published as little books—*The Spirit of the Common Law* (1921), *An Introduction to the Philosophy of Law* (1922), *Law and Morals* (1923), *Interpretations of Legal History* (1923), *The Formative Era of American Law* (1938), *The Development of Constitutional Guarantees of Liberty* (1957), and several others. In point of fact, the four chapters comprising *Social Control Through Law* constitute a series of lectures that Pound gave at Indiana University in 1941. He also delivered numerous addresses to bar associations and other public audiences in the United States, England, and on the Continent. Among the many accolades he acquired throughout his career, Pound received honorary doctorates from some sixteen universities at home and abroad. His accomplishments, however, were not limited to the halls of academe. Pound's nonacademic work included important practical aspects of law: international arbitrator to the American-British Claims Arbitration (1926–1927); consultant on administrative procedure and crime surveys, including the Cleveland Survey of Criminal Justice (1921–1922) and the Boston Crime Survey (1926); member of President Hoover's National Commission on Law Observance and Enforcement (the "Wickersham Commission"), which was concerned with the problems of national Prohibition (1929–1931); director of the National Conference of Judicial Councils (1938–1946); and advisor to the Chinese Nationalist government's Ministry of Justice, leaving for

Nanking to undertake the task of setting up the courts (1946–1949).

II

The intellectual influences that contributed, directly or indirectly, to Pound's juristic thought are too numerous to properly list here. However, particular mention should be made of two jurists, one philosopher, and three sociologists who had a indelible impact on Pound's thinking.

To begin with, two of Pound's major contributions to jurisprudence—the idea of historical relativity in law and the notion of jural postulates—were partly derived from the nineteenth-century neo-Hegelian jurist, Josef Kohler. The idea of historical relativity in law took form in Kohler as he looked at law not as a fixed and permanent entity suitable for all time, but as a dynamic phenomenon of human civilization. Kohler, in his *Philosophy of Law* (1914), maintained that since civilization is constantly developing and changing, so too must the law evolve and adapt to the changing needs and demands of culture. It follows, then, that for Kohler the law that is suitable for one period of civilization is not so for another.

For Pound as for Kohler, the task of the law is twofold: To maintain the existing values of civilization and to maintain, further, and transmit to their most complete possibilities the human powers of a given civilization. In *Social Control Through Law,* however, Pound goes beyond Kohler in arguing that the ideal civilization must recognize competition and cooperation as two factors in achieving ultimate mastery over external and internal human nature. In Pound's view, human beings need the force of social control to keep their aggressive, self-assertive side in balance with their cooperative social tendency. He recognized that despite the law's three distinct meanings—namely, that of legal order, the body of precepts, and the judicial/administrative process—they could all be united by the idea of social control. Consequently, Pound approached law as a type of organized social control, which he describes in *Social Control Through Law* as "the pressure upon each man brought to bear by his fellow men in order to constrain him to do his part in upholding civilized society and to deter him from antisocial conduct, that is, conduct at variance with the postulates of social order" (p. 18). Thus, for

Pound, the subject-matter of law involves examining those manifestations of internal nature which, in asserting or seeking to realize individual expectations, require social control.

The law, in turn, is shaped by civilization's requirements for certain definite principles of law that Pound and Kohler term the "jural postulates" of civilized life. But whereas Kohler fails to specifically explain how the jural postulates are determined and derived, Pound, as will be discussed presently, conceives them to be presupposed by the de facto claims, demands, or interests made by human beings. Once Pound arrived at a method for determining the jural postulates of a given time and place he then proceeded to connect them to his idea of the scheme of interests.

From Rudolf von Jhering, Pound appropriated the notion of interests—the purposes of human existence—which, when given individual expression are characterized by *egoistical* self-assertion, and when given social expression involve collective cooperation through *ethical* self-assertion. In *Law as a Means to an End* (1913) Jhering views the law as an instrument for securing the social interests, that is, the general, objective, and organized purposes of a number of people. What is more, for Jhering a legally protected interest is a legal right. From these ideas Pound was able to formulate what became his highly popular "theory of social interests." Jhering's regard for the de facto interests that are asserted in a particular civilization, had a considerable impact on Pound. Additionally, Pound drew from Jhering's concept of *purpose* in the law; of law owing its origins to a practical motive, to an end. Pound was attracted to the fact that Jhering inquired into the more immediate social purposes and functions of law, rather than what had previously been considered important in nineteenth-century jurisprudence: the abstract nature of law.

From William James's philosophy of pragmatism, Pound acquired the ethical position, stated in James's essay "The Moral Philosopher and the Moral Life" (1891), that the end of ends is the goal for satisfying at all times as many demands as possible. Pound modified this utilitarian consideration in two significant ways. First, Pound states that the task of law should be to, at all times, satisfy as much of the total amount as it can for as many demands as it can. Or, as he puts it in *Social Control*

Through Law, the law as a mechanism of social control "makes it possible to do the most
that can be done for the most people" (p. 64).
However, since all desired resources—that is,
the goods of existence, the scope for free activity, and the objects on which to exert free
activity—are limited, people's appetite for
goods and objects will inevitably conflict with
or overlap those of their neighbors. In this case,
Pound looks to the entire scheme of interests
in dealing with a multiplicity of competing interests of a given situation. Second, and in con-
tradistinction to James, Pound argues that
implicit in the balancing of social interests and
in the preservation of a pluralistic community's
stability is the problem of values: the question
of how to measure and appraise conflicting
and overlapping social interests. Throughout
his works, Pound repeatedly emphasizes that
no legal philosophy can escape the problem
of values. Indeed, Pound regards sociological
jurisprudence as a prescriptive and valuative
science. As such, his object is to give effect to
the greatest total of interests or to the interests
that weigh most in civilization, with the least
sacrifice to the scheme of interests as a whole.
However, in *Social Control Through Law*

Pound candidly admits that "[m]anifestly one cannot speak with assurance as to how we are in the end to value competing and overlapping interests in the present century" (p. 126).

Turning next to the sociological components of Pound's jurisprudence, it is widely recognized that they were derived largely from the writings of Lester F. Ward, Albion W. Small, and most especially E. A. Ross, who was a colleague of Pound's at the University of Nebraska during 1901–1906. Ward was an ardent advocate of government control and social planning who believed that legislation would contribute to the organization of human experience. Similarly, Small assumed that social reform could be carried out through legal means. Due to the influence of these two men Pound approached the law as a form of "social engineering." Indeed, the idea of law as an instrument of engineering and social control at all levels of government is an integral part of Pound's sociological jurisprudence. Toward the end of his life, Pound acknowledges his intellectual debts to Ross and Small in the preface to his magnum opus *Jurisprudence*. He writes: "Happily in the early years of the present century it was my good fortune to be associated with Edward A. Ross, then Professor at Nebraska, and thus to be set to reading Ward and to thinking about sociological jurisprudence. When I went to Chicago in 1907 I met Albion W. Small, and to Ross and Small,...I owe a decisive impetus at a critical point in my study."

In 1901 Ross published *Social Control,* a book that quickly became an early American classic, representing an elaborate inventory of the methods by which a society induces conformity into human behavior. Here Ross contends that of all the various instrumentalities of social control—public opinion, belief, social suggestion, religion, and so forth—law reigns supreme as "the most specialized and highly finished engine of control employed by society." Following Ross's lead, Pound thereafter focuses on the social character of law and sees the law, simultaneously, as reflecting the needs of a well-ordered society and as influencing that society. Accordingly, in *Social Control Through Law,* Pound defines law as a "highly specialized form of social control, carried on in accordance with a body of authoritative precepts, applied in a judicial and an administrative process" (p. 41). The upshot of Ross's influence is that the notion of social control provided Pound's jurisprudence with a sociological starting point.

In light of Pound's efforts to purposefully forge intellectual ties and cultivate personal friendships with such early American sociologists as Ward, Small, and Ross (as well as with Harvard sociologists and Pound's colleagues, Georges Gurvitch, Nicholas S. Timasheff, Pitirim Sorokin, and Talcott Parsons), it is ironic that Pound's work is now scarcely considered in the sociological community. Clearly, Pound's sociological jurisprudence is an applied science in the tradition of empirical sociology. In "Philosophy of Law and Comparative Law" (1951), Pound underscores his preference for this tradition and acknowledges sociology's influence on him in stating that he, like other scholars trained during the early twentieth century, had been educated on the empiricism and sociology of Auguste Comte. The cumulative effect of these sociological influences is that Pound's philosophy of law significantly promoted the recognition of law as a social phenomenon. Little wonder that Pound felt justified in referring to his legal philosophy as *sociological* jurisprudence.

III

The rise of Roscoe Pound's sociological jurisprudence is crucially interwoven with the vast institutional and ideological transformations taking place in the United States during the first quarter of the twentieth century. At this time the United States was shedding its frontier image and entering a period of modernity, an era characterized by increased urbanization (largely as a result of massive immigration) and industrialization. Rapid social change, triggered in part by enormous economic growth, helped the country achieve its status as a major world power. In the process, however, this rapid social change also generated immense social problems characterized by new and sharper levels of tension and conflict: poor working conditions in factories, political corruption, crowded city slums, the growth of the impoverished masses, the cartelization of the American economy, and the like.

Typically sluggish in keeping up with changing times, the American legal system entered the twentieth century in its traditional nineteenth-century guise, as formalist or analytical jurisprudence. Clearly the most pervasively influential school of jurisprudence, analytical jurisprudence was the most recent school at the time that Pound was writing. Austin—Pound's inspiration while a law student—was a key figure in nineteenth-century analytical jurisprudence as he suggested the development of a formal, logical closed system of law. The five schools of jurists and methods of jurisprudence that preceded the analytical school and that Pound details in *The Spirit of the Common Law* are the metaphysical school, the historical school, the utilitarians, the positivists, and the mechanical sociologists.

Analytical jurisprudence, being politically congruent with the liberal political theory of the post-Civil War period, had kept legal intervention and regulation in social and economic matters to a bare minimum. This laissez-faire policy did not signify the complete absence of legal oversight, it merely meant shifting the responsibility of control from artificial entities like the polity to "natural" ones like the marketplace. The self-regulating market was said to be guided by such universal economic principles as occupational specialization, the growth of wealth, and self-interest.

The notion of universal, or first, principles—that is, fixed axioms, eternal truths, predetermined conceptions—also affected the academic disciplines of biology, economics, and sociology. Indeed, during the nineteenth century there was an intense preoccupation with the idea that general absolutes governed the social and natural worlds; thus, it was only a matter of time before American legal doctrine was likewise attracted to the universal principle. However, not long into the new century the natural and social sciences—namely, biology, economics, sociology—made an abrupt about-face and abandoned the attempt to deduce knowledge from predetermined conceptions. In contrast, analytical jurisprudence tenaciously held on to the traditional notion of authoritative precepts and this made the law rigid and unyielding. Noting the law's inability to keep up with social progress, in his 1910 article, "Law in Books and Law in Action," Pound wryly observed that the law had always been dominated by ideas of the past long after they had ceased being vital in other knowledge-fields. Accordingly, legal doctrine ran into the problem of not being able to adapt to the changing social and economic conditions of the time. Or, as Pound saw it, there existed a discrepancy between the law in books and the law in action. The traditional legal doctrine revealed its inadequacy by failing to meet social ends. As Pound succinctly states in *Social Control Through Law,* law "falls short of what is expected of it, especially in dealing with the many new questions and endeavors to secure newly pressing interests involved in a changing economic order" (p. 14).

Pound introduced sociological jurisprudence in a revolutionary address that he delivered in St. Paul, Minnesota, on August 29, 1906, before that most staid of legal bodies, the American Bar Association. He stated resolutely that the American court system was archaic and its legal procedures behind the times. Pound's speech was a clarion call for the reform and modernization of what he saw as an antiquated system of legal justice. Law, he remarked in characteristically bold fashion, usually functions as a government of the living by the dead. This speech was pivotal in American legal history because it marked the beginning of a new movement in law that shook, challenged, and disturbed the existing system of legal orthodoxy. As John Wigmore so eloquently put it, Pound's

St. Paul speech was the "spark that kindled the white flame" of legal progress.

In his 1908 article, "Mechanical Jurisprudence," Pound commented on the need for a scientific law. For Pound the word "scientific" had two distinct meanings: one refers to the art of abstract systematization, the other to the technique of pragmatic application. He states that analytical jurisprudence had transformed law into a reasoned body of principles for the administration of justice. Analytical jurisprudence is scientific in the abstract sense because it is marked by a conformity to reason, uniformity, and certainty. As such, law is endowed with a certain degree of logic, precision, and predictability. Put another way, as a deductive system of law, analytical jurisprudence is scientific in that it reduces judges' biases, ignorance, and possibility of corruption preventing their departure from clearly articulated, predetermined rules. Pound, however, favored the notion of scientific law in its pragmatic sense. Thus, he points out the shortcomings of a jurisprudence that is abstractly scientific as concerns the logical processes of its internal structure but not concerning the practical results it achieves. According to Pound, since analytical jurisprudence regarded the law not as a means to a achieving an empirical end but as a means in itself, it had transformed lawmaking and judicial adjudication into a technical and artificial enterprise. Moreover, Pound notes that owing to the law's artificiality, lawyers tend to forget that the real function of scientific law is to adjust everyday relations so as to meet current ideas of fair play. Additionally, the rigid exposition of hard-and-fast rules in analytical jurisprudence prevents the law from adapting itself to the mutable culture of a modern, urban environment. As a result, the law had ceased having a utilitarian function in dealing with the realities of everyday life. It had turned into a hopelessly self-sustaining entity completely out of touch with the human condition and the new social needs that had arisen within the past half century.

Analytical jurisprudence, with its a priori concepts and deductive calculus, had become a mechanical jurisprudence. Pound urges jurists to reject the technical operations of mechanical legal doctrine, or what he sometimes referred to as "the jurisprudence of conceptions," and accept a more realistic and action-oriented "jurisprudence of ends." The central question to be considered, according to Pound, should be: How will a rule or decision operate in practice? His objective in asking it is to attain a pragmatic, sociological legal science that would make rules fit cases instead of making cases fit rules. In short, Pound's sociological jurisprudence—which regarded the actual operation of law rather than its abstract content—was a protest against the conceptualist jurisprudence prevalent among early twentieth-century judges.

In 1907, in his address to the American Bar Association's Section on Legal Education, Pound advanced the idea that the artificial and technical nature of mechanical jurisprudence had created a discrepancy between the conceptualism of the written law and the more sublunary sentiments of the American public. That is to say, that the law's rigidity prevents it from considering the practical needs, wants, and interests of the individuals the law is meant to serve. Accordingly, Pound maintained that American legal theory and doctrine had reached a degree of "fixity" prior to the emergence of the conditions that the law must address in a modern, urban, industrial society. However, in "The Need of a Sociological Jurisprudence" (1907), he notes optimistically that with the rise and growth of economics, political science, and sociology the time was ripe for a new tendency in legal scholarship that would consider the practical relations of law to society. A few years later, in "The Scope and Purpose of Sociological Jurisprudence," a lengthy three-part article that appeared in the 1911 and 1912 issues of the *Harvard Law Review,* Pound announced the emergence of sociological jurisprudence as a discrete and definable legal philosophy. Pound's sociological jurisprudence treats law not as a conceptual and logical system of formal rules, but as an institution operating within a larger societal context that functions to regulate social processes with the object of securing and protecting society's interests. With this notion of law Pound, through the theory of social interests, explains how the law accomplishes this objective. However, before the theory of social interests can be discussed, the jural postulates of time and place must be analyzed.

IV

Inspired by Kohler, who in Hegelian fashion stressed the ideal rather than the nonrational elements of the civilization of a given period, Pound ultimately formulated a total of seven jural ideals or postulates that provided him with an organizing framework within which to locate his scheme of interests. In broad view, the jural postulates are a set of fundamental presuppositions that encompass the moral sentiments of a reflective community and that are recognized and enforced by law concerning reasonable expectations of human conduct in a civilized society of the time and place. By "civilized society" Pound has in mind the English-speaking countries of Great Britain, the United States, Canada, Australia, and New Zealand. The deliberate exclusion of countries that did not develop their legal systems according to the conventions of English common law clearly reveals Pound's bias in favor of the Anglo-American legal tradition. Thus, at the present time when the ideas of cultural diversity and cultural equality have gained hegemony in the arts, humanities, and social sciences, Pound's remarks about the legal order of the civilized society of the time and place appear to be ethnocentric at best.

The jural postulates are expressed as expectations, claims, or "rights" and are procured from the great substantive branches of the positive law including criminal law, the law of torts (especially negligence and liability without fault), property law, contract law, and the law of restitution. The first five jural postulates for the domain of American law, at least, are articulated in Chapter IV of *Social Control Through Law* as follows:

1. In civilized society men must be able to assume that others will commit no intentional aggressions upon them.
2. In civilized society men must be able to assume that they control for beneficial purposes what they have discovered and appropriated to their own use, what they have created by their own labor, and what they have acquired under the existing social and economic order.
3. In civilized society men must be able to assume that those with whom they deal in the general intercourse of society will act in good faith and hence

   (a) will make good reasonable expectations which their promises or other conduct reasonably create;

(b) will carry out their undertakings according to the expectations which the moral sentiment of the community attaches thereto;

(c) will restore specifically or by equivalent what comes to them by mistake or unanticipated situation whereby they receive, at another's expense, what they could not reasonably have expected to receive under the actual circumstances.

4. In civilized society men must be able to assume that those who are engaged in some course of conduct will act with due care not to cast an unreasonable risk of injury upon others.

5. In civilized society men must be able to assume that those who maintain things likely to get out of hand or to escape and do damage will restrain them or keep them within their proper bounds.

In recognition of the two main directions that juristic thinking was taking—(1) concern for the concrete individual life rather than for the abstract individual will, and (2) concern for civilization as distinct from and contrasted with politically organized society—Pound, in 1959, proposed two new jural postulates in the first volume of his *Jurisprudence*:

6. Everyone is entitled to assume that the burdens incident to life in society will be borne by society.

7. Everyone is entitled to assume that at least a standard human life will be assured him; not merely equal opportunities of providing or attaining it, but immediate material satisfactions.

As social-ethical principles, the jural postulates for law have a practical three-fold purpose. First, they are meant to identify and explain the substantial totality of actual human claims, demands, or interests of a given social order. Second, they express what the majority of individuals in a given society want the law to do. Third, and relatedly, the jural postulates are meant to guide the courts in applying the law. Pound asserts that the jural postulates are neither eternal, immutable, or exhaustive. Indeed, he regards them as principles that overlap, conflict, and are in continuous dynamic transition. Pound's position toward the jural postulates is therefore one of relativity, for upon being recognized the postulates are legally protected only until the empirical facts of a changing society make them outmoded and obsolete. In the meantime, they are employed in the practical work of bringing a particular society's legal institutions into a condition of harmony with the jural postulates, and therefore into a condition of harmony with the de facto claims made by the majority of persons in a given society at a given time.

The link between the jural postulates and the scheme of interests is less than clear in Pound's work. In *Social Control Through Law* he treats the jural postulates as simply a method for valuating social interests, one that was fast becoming less useful because society was undergoing the transition to a social order that had not yet formulated a generally accepted notion of the ideal. In *Jurisprudence,* by contrast, Pound refers to the jural postulates and the scheme of interests as two approaches that he finds useful in teaching law. In other contexts, Pound views the jural postulates as nothing more than general and universal expressions of the social interests. In any event,

Pound does see a need for some connection, a mediating procedure, between the practical problems posed by the administration of justice and the jural postulates of the civilization of the time and place. This link consists of a set of interests which, like the jural postulates, also press for legal recognition and enforcement in that society. Pound rather ingeniously classifies certain claims of human beings to have things and do things by distinguishing between three ideal type interests: the individual, the public, and the social.

V

In Chapter III of *Social Control Through Law* Pound defines an interest as "a demand or desire which human beings, either individually or through groups or associations or in relations, seek to satisfy." Individual interests, he tells us, are "claims or demands or desires involved immediately in the individual life and asserted in title of that life." Individual interests divide into interests in personality, interests in domestic relations, and interests of substance. Public interests consist of "claims or demands or desires involved in life in a politically organized society and asserted in title of that organization." Finally, Pound defines social interests as "claims or demands or desires involved in social life in civilized society and asserted in title of that life" (quotations from pp. 66 and 69). Pound warns that these three types of interests are overlapping and interdependent and that most claims, demands, and desires can be placed in all three categories, depending upon one's purpose. However, as a practical matter, and in order to compare them on the same plane, he tended to treat claims, demands, and desires in their most general form, that is, as social interests.

It is no exaggeration to say that Pound's theory of social interests is crucial to his thinking about law and lies at the conceptual core of sociological jurisprudence. Pound first presented the theory in the keynote address which he delivered before the American Sociological Society in 1920. Considering that Pound's notion of social interests evolved through the years, a composite description derived from Chapter III of *Social Control Through Law,* "A Survey of Social Interests" (1943), and the third volume of Pound's *Jurisprudence* (1959), yields the following definition: *Social interests are the prevalent and reasonable, de facto claims, demands, desires, or expectations that human beings collectively seek to satisfy and that civilized society must recognize and protect through law.* Because law protects social interests they are given the status of legal rights. Thus, a right is usually a legally protected social interest. In *Social Control Through Law* Pound explains that the relation between interests and rights has to do with the fact that the latter conception is plagued with a multiplicity of meanings. At bottom, however, Pound rejects the idea of rights as being natural or inalienable—a quality inherent in humans as rational beings. Pound argues that what is natural are not "rights" but "interests."

In contrast to the abstract idea of right, social interests are strictly and precisely empirical entities because they are to be found solely in the law and legal processes of society. In other words, social interests are not abstruse propositions derived, through logical deduction, from such determinist sources as theological doctrine, philosophical ideas about human nature, or the psychological classification of instincts. Rather, social interests can be inferred only through the empirical investigation of such objective data as court decisions, legislative declarations, and what is written in a wide array of works (most of which, for Pound, are Western and especially English and American sources) referring to the law. In "A Survey of Social Interests," Pound explains that the first step in conducting such an investigation involves surveying the legal order (by which he means the regime maintained by a mature system of law in the latest stage of its development) and inventorying those social interests that have pressed upon lawmakers, judges, and jurists for recognition and satisfaction. Through a painstaking and thorough analysis of hundreds of legal documents, Pound inventories the social interests that have been asserted and which must be acknowledged and secured by the courts in order to maintain social order and attain civilized society. He proposes six broad categories of social interests and their subcategories:

I. *The social interest in general security* refers to society's claim to be secure against those patterns of behavior that threaten its existence. This social interest takes five forms:

1. *Physical safety of the people.*

2. *General health of the population.*
3. *Peace and public order.*
4. *Security of acquisitions,* or the demands that titles are not vulnerable to indefinite attack.
5. *Security of transactions,* or the demands that previous commercial exchanges are not subject to indefinite inquiry, so as to unsettle credit and disturb business and trade.

II. *The social interest in security of social institutions* refers to society's claim that its fundamental institutions be secure from patterns of behavior that threaten their existence or impair their efficient functioning. This social interest takes four forms:

1. *Security of domestic institutions.*
2. *Security of religious institutions.*
3. *Security of political institutions.*
4. *Security of economic institutions.*

III. *The social interest in general morals* refers to society's claim to be secure against patterns of behavior deemed offensive to the moral sentiments of the general population.

IV. *The social interest in conservation of social resources* refers to society's claim that the goods of existence not be needlessly and completely wasted. This social interest takes two forms:

1. *Use and conservation of natural resources.*

2. *Protection and training of dependents and defectives.*

V. *The social interest in general progress* refers to society's claim that the development of human powers and of human control over nature for the satisfaction of human wants go forward. This social interest takes three forms:

1. *Economic progress.*

2. *Political progress.*

3. *Cultural progress.*

VI. *The social interest in individual life* refers to society's claim that each individual be able to live a human life in accordance with the standards of the society. This social interest takes three forms:

1. *Individual self-assertion.* (This claim is expressed in those cases where self-help is allowed).

2. *Individual opportunity* refers to society's claim that all individuals have fair, reasonable, and equal opportunities.

3. *Individual conditions of life* refers to the claim that each individual be assured at

least the minimum living conditions which society can provide at that point in time.

Although Pound compiled this inventory of social interests between 1920 and 1959 with the intent of identifying the prevailing claims of his era, he was well aware of the fact that new values would emerge in the future. While he paid scant attention to predicting what interests *will* be recognized, he nonetheless seems to have foreshadowed claims that clamored for recognition and protection by American legislatures, courts, and administrative agencies during the 1960s and beyond. In *Social Control Through Law,* Pound states with some foresight: "But some part of the path of the juristic thought of tomorrow is already apparent. It seems to be a path toward an ideal of cooperation rather than one of competitive self-assertion" (pp. 126–27). These claims of the 1960s, which developed out of the exigencies of particular political and moral struggles, were, to a measured degree, based on values of cooperation, stimulated in part by the principles of greater equality, tolerance, and social justice. In the zeitgeist of the 1960s,

the claims, incited by a spirit of "cooperation"—expressed, for example, as "peace and
love" by some leaders of the youth movement
and by "understanding" by some leaders of the
civil rights movement—were given voice by
public opinion, public policies, and court
decisions.

Numerous social interests, which many believed ought to be protected and promoted by
procedures of law and government, were re-
alized through the civil rights movement; the
Warren Court's most significant decisions
including the school segregation cases; the
Johnson administration's war on poverty and
war on crime; social welfare policies and pro-
grams like aid to dependent children, Medic-
aid and Medicare; the Civil Rights Act of 1964;
consumer protection legislation; questions of
civil liberties; affirmative action; protections
against self-incrimination; the environmental
movement and energy crisis. While Pound
would probably have endorsed these claims
(though perhaps not the immediacy and ur-
gency with which they were made), it is highly
unlikely that, despite his intensely activist drive,
he would have approved of the political methods employed in publicizing the claims and

reforming the laws suppressing them. Riots, boycotts, strikes, protests, and other types of "antisocial conduct" are largely incompatible with Pound's efforts at social engineering which demanded the "weighing," "balancing," and "ordering"—the reconciliation and harmonizing—of conflicting and overlapping social interests for achieving stability of the social order.

VI

Pound's juristic thinking has not aged well through the years. One reason for this is that, like many persuasive intellectuals, Pound became a victim of his own success. Indeed, at the height of his long career from the middle of the first decade to the 1940s, his focus on the ends of law and his rejection of formalism were readily embraced by many jurists, including, and especially, the legal realists. This general acceptance of Pound's concepts within a generation or so after they were proposed made them outdated and "obvious." His ideas quickly became so commonplace and an integral part of the legal culture that they soon ceased to be seen as pioneering or heretical. This is not to say that Pound's sociological jurisprudence is devoid of concepts with enduring value; it is to say that there have been few attempts to extend or revise his ideas. For example, research on the role of interests in formulating and administering law has been virtually nonexistent.

Concerning this latter point, Pound was again a victim, a victim of unpropitious timing. Toward the end of his life when he published his massive *Jurisprudence,* a five-volume work consolidating the sociological interpretations of law and legal ideas that had occupied Pound throughout his career, a new model of society was taking shape in sociology. The conflict model, initially inspired by the works of by C. Wright Mills, Ralf Dahrendorf, Lewis Coser, and other social theorists writing during the late 1950s, began to supplant the consensus or pluralistic model that had been popular since World War II. The conflict theorists argued for a critical analysis of society and its institutions. They tended to view society, not as being characterized by consensus and stability, but by diversity, conflict, and coercion. They also regarded law, not as an instrument that functions outside of interests to resolve conflicts between interests, but as a *consequence* of the operation of interests. These two tenets directly challenged the political and moral assumptions of Pound's sociological jurisprudence and most especially his theory of social interests, both of which are premised on a pluralistic model of society that, rather benignly, and perhaps also naively, assumes that the legal order is created in society solely for the purpose of adjusting relations and ordering conduct. Jurists, legal sociologists, critical criminologists, and other scholars influenced by the conflict model—and several of its variants stemming from the New Left movement, social-conflict theory, the Frankfurt School, the various Marxisms, and, since the late 1970s, critical legal studies—have taken a radically different view of law and society. In general, these critical theorists maintain that law is not the product of the whole society nor does it serve those interests that are good for the whole society. Rather, for them, law incorporates the interests of a power elite—those specific persons and groups with the power to translate their interests into public policy. Thus, contrary to Pound's pluralistic conception of politics, law does not represent a compromise of diverse interests in society, but supports some interests at the expense of others. By the early 1960s Pound's theory of social interests was no longer given even passing consideration by sociologists and jurists. What the legal philosopher Julius Stone referred to as "the Golden Age of Pound" had, by that time, virtually faded into obscurity.

In addition, it must be said that while Pound's theory of interests provides fairly objective criteria for assessing the legal orders of the United States, Great Britain, and other English-speaking countries from which he drew his data, it offers far less for the comparative evaluation of countries uninfluenced by Anglo-American common law. Thus, in the age of the global village, Pound's theory seems to be seriously lacking in broad, multicultural explanatory power. Finally, and in fairness to Pound, it should be acknowledged that while he failed to produce a clear body of tenets, a rigorous set of methodologies or propositions about legal theory, there is one dominant intellectual theme that two of the most influential twentieth-century schools of jurisprudence—American legal realism and critical legal studies—trace directly to Pound: that the law had come to be out of touch with reality.

VII

Social Control Through Law is a remarkable book in manner and style. Here Pound adopts an admonishing tone from time to time, but his admonition is never overbearing as it is always tempered by polite regard for the positions of others. He gently (some may say, too gently) critiques the ideas of Hans Kelsen, Oliver Wendell Holmes, the legal realists, and others without mentioning them by name. Although he forcefully, and often persuasively, advances his ideas, Pound avoids crossing the line into callous dogmatism and polemics. Moreover, while he usually writes in generalities, and this is particularly the case with books like *Social Control Through Law* which were originally delivered as lectures, Pound, nonetheless, exemplifies his remarks with instances of actual legal practice. One contemporary aspect of *Social Control Through Law* is aptly demonstrated by our postmodern society and its skyrocketing rate of litigation. Now that the familial and religious institutions have lost much of their influence, the courts exert an unprecedented degree of control over the public and private lives of most Americans. To an extent perhaps unimagined by Pound, law remains the paramount agency of social control. In short, *Social Control Through Law* is an insightful, concise summary of Pound's ideas that, after more than half a century, remains surprisingly fresh and relevant. It will doubtless continue to engage jurists, legal theorists, and sociologists for many years to come.

A. JAVIER TREVIÑO
April 1996

SOCIAL CONTROL
THROUGH LAW

I

CIVILIZATION AND SOCIAL CONTROL

WILLIAM JAMES is reported to have said that the worst enemies of any subject are the professors thereof. In saying this he had reference to practical activities such as medicine and law. In these the practitioner is in constant contact with the facts of life and of nature. He arrives at his ideas from experience and must constantly revise his ideas and recast his theories to meet the facts to which they must be applied. The professor, on the other hand, takes facts and life and nature from the relations of others and assumes them as something given him. He generalizes from them and formulates conceptions and theories from which he deduces further conceptions and theories, and upon them he builds a body of teaching which is obstinate, resistant to the facts of life and nature and very persistent, and seeks to make life and nature conform to his theoretical model. There is a warning for us who are busied

with the social sciences in this dictum. To
speak only of my own special field, it is
certainly true as we look back that the
judges and practitioners of fifty years ago
were well in advance of the jurists and
teachers in what have proved to be the
significant movements in law. Everywhere
the science of law lagged behind the actual
course of legislation and judicial decision.
So far as it had practical effect it obstructed.
Most of what we now complain of in the
judical decisions as to social legislation in
the last generation represented what was
taught as the up-to-date science of jurisprudence. The pressure of unrecognized,
partially recognized, unsecured, or insuf-
ficiently secured interests often put the
actual law of the nineteenth century well in
advance of the juristic theory of the time.

There are two elements in the body of
precepts which make up a system of law,
an imperative element and a traditional
element. The former is the work of the lawmaker. The philosopher commonly offers
him guidance. But he is likely to think of
himself as invested with a power of command. The latter is the product of experi-

ence. At Rome it grew out of the experience of jurisconsults in answering questions as to actual controversies litigated in the forum. In our law it has grown out of experience in the decision of cases in the courts and the endeavor of judges to find in recorded judicial experience the principles of deciding new questions arising in concrete controversies. Thus we have law as command and law as ascertainment and formulation of the just on the basis of experience. Each seeks to establish just precepts. Each, therefore, is governed by some ideal. In the eighteenth century, and with us in the fore part of the nineteenth century, the ideal was provided both for legislature and for judge by the theory of natural law, a theory of a body of ideal precepts of universal validity for all peoples, all times, and all places, derived from ideas of what an ideal man would do and would not do, would claim and would concede as the claims of others, and arrived at by pure reason.

Philosophy was in its heyday as the guide of law in the reign of natural law both in the classical era of Roman law and in the law of Europe and America in the seventeenth and eighteenth centuries. Every law book had a philosophical introduction, and great acts of legislation often had a philosophical preamble. But, apart from philosophical difficulties with the theory, natural law failed to maintain itself as a workable instrument of making and finding the law. While it professed to be ideal and universal, derived from universal reason, it was in fact, as I have been in the habit of putting it, a positive, not a natural, natural law. It was an idealized version of the positive law of the time and place so that in practice the law was made to provide the critique of itself. For example, when the British set up a court at Penang and had to administer justice to a community which had no law, it was held that the court was to be governed by natural law. But when Lord Westbury in the Judicial Committee of the Privy Council came to apply natural law to an appeal from such a court, it turned out that the universal natural law was the same even in details as the law of England.

In the latter part of the nineteenth century, with the breakdown of natural law, we sought, particularly in the English-

speaking world, to get on without philosophy. There was the fact that certain
precepts were applied by the courts and had
behind them ultimately the sheriff and his
posse. They had received the guinea stamp
of the state, and were backed by the force of
politically organized society. Here was
something we could tie to. These precepts
were the pure fact of law. Nothing that did
not have this guinea stamp and was not
backed by force was to be considered by the
scientific jurist. But we had to learn from
the courts and the practitioners that this
pure fact of law was an illusion. They could
not ignore an ideal element in law even if
the jurist had thrown it out. Whenever they
were called on to choose between equally
authoritative starting points for reasoning,
whenever they were called on to interpret
the text of a legal precept, whenever they
were called on to apply a standard to conduct, the courts went outside the jurist's
pure fact of law and adjusted their determination to an ideal. Thus natural law had to
come back again at the beginning of the
present century, though not always with
that name and not this time as giving us a

universal code of ideal precepts. Its task now was not to give us an ideal body of universal legislation but to give us a critique of the ideal element in the positive law. Even if absolute ideals could not be proved, it could ascertain and formulate the social ideal of the time and place and make it a measure for choosing starting points for reasoning, of interpretation, and of applying standards. As it was put, we could have a natural law with a changing or a growing content.

Thus there came to be a revival of philosophy of law in the fore part of the present century. About the same time sociology, the science of society, founded by Comte a hundred years ago, had made its place among the social sciences and a sociology of law sprang up alongside of social philosophies of law. But here, too, the teachers have been going their way with too little knowledge of the problems with which the administration of justice has to wrestle and often with too little grasp of the experience developed by reason which is formulated in the traditional element of legal systems. Hence we have had to develop a philosophical science of law, a philosophical jurisprudence, and a sociological jurisprudence. We call on philosophy, ethics, politics, and sociology to help, but to help in what are regarded as problems of jurisprudence. We study law in all of its senses as a much specialized phase of what in a larger view is a science of society.

Philosophical juristic theories have been worked out as solutions of particular problems of a time and then put in universal form and made to do service for all the problems of the legal order everywhere. What we require is not a philosophy of law that seeks to force law into the bed of Procrustes of its system, nor a sociology of law that runs to methodology and seeks to justify a science of society by showing that it has its own special method by which then all the phenomena of social life are to be tried, but a sociology that knows how to use philosophy and a sociological jurisprudence that knows how to use social philosophy and a philosophical sociology.

Looking back over forty years of the present century we see that much has been accomplished. Stammler revived what the

French call juridical idealism. If he did not give us the solution he showed us the problem. He sought to make us conscious of the ideal element in the positive law and to construct a theory of it, where nineteenth-century natural law had sought a critique; just as Kant before him had sought to establish principles of lawmaking where his predecessors had sought to find a universal code. Duguit gave us a theory of an urban industrial society of the beginning of the present century as a theory of the ideal element of the law of today. His is a sociological natural law. He conceived of everything in law as deriving its validity from and to be judged by a fundamental principle of right-and-law. Following Comte he sought to arrive at it by observation and verify it by further observation. In fact, he did his observing in Durkheim's book on the division of labor in society. Duguit's vogue is not what it was. But he has had a useful influence. Gény showed us the importance of the technique element in positive law and gave us a Neo-Scholastic theory of the ideal element. His *Science et technique en droit privé positif* has by no means been appreciated as it deserves. It deals with what seems to me a fundamental problem of jurisprudence, namely, the measure of valuing interests, and with two elements of law which the analytical jurisprudence of the last century ignored, and treats them in an original and suggestive way. Hauriou gave us a theory of the organizations which are significant agencies of social control in the society of today. At bottom, his theory, a Neo-Scholastic institutionalism, seems to me an attempt to understand and construct a theory of the labor organizations which are the most active groups in the society of today, and in the English-speaking world have been coming to be the dominant element both in employing extra-legal force in a time when the state was supposed to have a monopoly of force and in harnessing the force of politically organized society to their purposes. The multiplicity of what he calls institutions—things established with a continuous existence apart from any persons for the time being, certain of whose activities are organized without their personalities being included, and setting up organs of authority and procedures of their own—this

multiplicity of institutions, each carrying out
its own idea, is to replace the crowd of
individuals, each exerting his will in a
never-ending conflict or competition, actual
or potential, which Kant sought to order. It
is significant that here we have a theory
which finds the unit elsewhere than in the
individual man, and that this theory has been
very generally accepted by writers on public
law at a time when that subject is crowding
private law even in the English-speaking
world in which the private-law view of
public law has been traditional. Before this
Ehrlich had shown us the significance in
society of relations and groups and associations and of their inner order as the basis of
the legal order. His idea of this inner order
of relations and groups and associations
should be compared with what the economic
determinist sees as imposition of the will of
the socially dominant class. His conception
of a complex of social facts involved in the
relations and associations which go to make
up human society deserves to be compared
with Duguit's observed and verified fact of
social interdependence in an economic order.
His idea of the reaction of living law, as he

calls it, upon generalizations and formulas, and of precepts and formulas which no longer reflect the inner order of significant relations and associations, should be compared with the view of the skeptical realists who can see nothing but individual behavior tendencies of individual judges. He made a significant beginning of a sociological comparative law or a comparative sociological jurisprudence which is palpably developing.

It is instructive to compare Ehrlich and Hauriou with ideas which obtained in antiquity as well as with the ideas of the nineteenth century. The Romans seem at one period to have thought of the individual man as a group. They could conceive of a one-individual household. One might be *paterfamilias*, patriarchal head of a household consisting of himself only. This, of course, goes back to a kin-organized society in which the kin group was the unit, from which the society of antiquity was emerging or had but lately emerged. In a society in which the individual is the unit we have been brought up to think of a group or association as an aggregate of individuals;

and in law we had thought of an association as an artificial individual. It was as hard for the last century to think of a group or association as it was for antiquity to think of a single individual. That we must think once more of relations and groups and associations, Gierke and Ehrlich and Hauriou make us realize. Indeed, Marx's theory of class struggle set thought of another type in the same direction. Durkheim's sociology and Duguit's doctrine of social interdependence through division of labor, where individual independence and the significance of the free individual will had been the central idea of the science of law in the nineteenth century, point also toward the rise of what might be called an institutional order, something with which the Italian idea of the corporative state, in which the legal unit is not the individual but the occupational group, must also be compared. All of these, from different standpoints, are theories of the urban, industrial society of today put universally.

These attempts to draw for us an accurate picture of society as it is must necessarily precede the philosophical critique of the received ideal which is part of the positive law. They are necessary in order to give us what idealized becomes the picture to which we refer our problems of adjusting relations and ordering conduct. When some one of these or some one of like kind which supersedes them becomes the received, authoritative picture, traditionally taught to lawyers and received by the profession and so by the judges and administrative officials, it will become the ideal element for the time being in the positive law. It is instructive to see how ideals of the social order, made to serve for ideals of the legal order and carried into detail as an ideal element in law, have gradually changed with changes in the social order they portray. Medieval law functioned in a relationally organized society in which the end of law seemed to be a harmonious maintaining of the social *status quo*. Medieval society, like the society of the Greek city-state, had no place for free competitive self-assertion. An ideal of this sort of society may be seen persisting long after the breakdown of the relationally organized feudal society. Slowly after the sixteenth century an ideal of a society of freely competing independent individuals grows up following the development of the modern economic order and replaces in juristic thought and legal tradition the ideal derived from antiquity and established in the Middle Ages. This newer ideal was fully developed in the nineteenth century. Indeed, its conception of a maximum of individual free self-assertion was put by Kant as a formulation of what we came to call legal justice. But the society which was pictured in the received ideal of the last century was in transition before the century was out and the ideal is slowly, if obstinately, giving way.

Law today throughout the world labors under a difficulty which explains much of the attack upon legal institutions and justice according to law which has been manifest for a generation. People are dissatisfied with law and are willing to try experiments in government without law because they feel that, as one might put it, law has not been operating lawfully. It falls short of what is expected of it, especially in dealing with the many new questions and endeavors to secure newly pressing interests involved in a changing economic order. This results from the failure of the received ideal to furnish satisfactory adjustments of conflicting and overlapping interests as they are presented to the courts today. We are properly dissatisfied with the picture of the self-sufficient individual in an economically self-sufficient neighborhood and freely competing with his neighbors in an economic order based on free competitive acquisition. This ideal governed in the last century and was easily adapted to a pioneer, rural, agricultural society. We know very well that it is not a true picture of the society of today. But we cannot see an exact picture of that society to take the place of the old picture. Perhaps the change has not yet gone far enough so we can draw the new picture. Hence the solution of new legal problems is very much at large. The force of politically organized society is left to itself. With no authoritative ideal to guide it, exercise of that force becomes a matter of individual wish and prejudice and predisposition—the very things law seeks to repress. A regime of force tries to do the work of a regime of law. If we are inclined to think badly of the regime of law as it operated in the last years of the nineteenth century, we cannot but see that it achieved much more toward civilization than the regime of force is achieving today.

This somewhat long introduction has seemed necessary in order to show why I am approaching law from the side of its ideal element and why I begin with the ideas of civilization, of social control as the means of maintaining civilization, and of law as an agency, or, in one sense of the term, a phase of social control.

Whether we think of civilization as fact or as idea it seems to me to be the starting point for the social sciences. Civilization has been said to be the raising of human powers to their highest possible unfolding. Thus there is a process, a condition to which the process has brought us thus far, and an idea of the process and the condition to which the process leads. But this way of putting it is too much in the manner of Hegel for the present generation. Let us say, then, the development of human powers to constantly greater completeness, the maximum of human control over external or physical nature and over internal or human nature of which men are for the time being capable.

These two sides of civilization are interdependent. If it were not for the control over internal nature which men have achieved they could have done little toward the conquest of external nature. If men had to go about armed and in constant fear of attack, if it were not a postulate that in civilized society men must be able to assume that others will commit no intentional aggression upon them, and that those who are engaged in a course of conduct will carry it on with due care not to cast an unreasonable risk of injury upon their fellows, it would not be possible to carry on the research and experiment and investigation which have made possible the harnessing of so much of physical nature to man's use. But without the control over physical nature which has been achieved it would not be possible for the enormous populations which now occupy the earth to maintain themselves. Thus the control over internal nature has enabled man to inherit the earth and to maintain and increase that inheritance. The social sciences have to do with this achieved mastery over internal or human nature—what it is, how it has come about, and above all how it is and may be maintained, furthered, and transmitted.

Immediately it is maintained by social control, by the pressure upon each man brought to bear by his fellow men in order to constrain him to do his part in upholding civilized society and to deter him from anti-social conduct, that is, conduct at variance with the postulates of the social order. The major agencies of social control are morals, religion, and law. In the beginnings of law these are not differentiated. Even in so advanced a civilization as that of the Greek city-state the same word is used to mean religious rites, ethical custom, the traditional course of adjusting relations, the legislation of the city, and all of these looked on as a whole; as we should say, including all these agencies of social control under the one term which we now translate law. So little was there in the way of differentiation that in a dialogue attributed to Plato, Socrates is made to speak of a gardener's manual as the laws of horticulture and a cookbook as the laws of cookery because the traditional rules of gardeners and cooks seemed generically like those of priests and moralists and judges

and legislators who declared authoritatively
the customs of the city. What we call public
opinion is a modern form of ethical custom
and is organized in all manner of voluntary
associations. When the development of
ethics gives rise to systems of morals there
is a stage of legal development in which
attempt is made to identify the legal with
the moral, to make all moral precepts as such
legal precepts also. Organized religion is by
no means the least of the major agencies.
For a long time in the history of civilization
it carries the greater part of the burden of
social control. Much of the beginnings of
law took over religious institutions and
religious precepts and put the force of the
state behind them. In the beginnings of
English law we find one of the Anglo-Saxon
kings exhorting his people as Christians to
keep the peace instead of commanding them
to do so as subjects. On the downfall of the
Roman empire in the West the church was
the chief agency of social control for some
six centuries, and in the later Middle Ages
the courts of the church and law of the church
divided jurisdiction over adjustment of relations and ordering conduct not unequally

with the courts of the state. Religion still has an intimate relation to the ideal element in law and one of the leading jurists of today tells us that for our measure of values, which he considers philosophy cannot give us, we must turn to religion.

In the modern world, law has become the paramount agency of social control. Our main reliance in the society of today is upon the force of politically organized society. We seek to adjust relations and order conduct through the orderly and systematic application of that force. At the moment this side of the law, its dependence upon force, is the one most insisted on. But it is well to remember that if law as a mode of social control has all the strength of force, it has also all the weakness of dependence on force. Moreover, that something very like law can exist and prove effective without any backing of force is shown by the achievements of international law from the seventeenth century to the last World War.

In a kin-organized society, a society in which the unit was not the individual human being but instead a group of kindred, the task of the law was a simple one of keeping the peace among warring groups. If one kinsman injured another, the internal discipline of the kin group took care of the matter. If a member of one kin group injured a member of another, there was no common superior to adjust the resulting controversy and the blood feud was a usual result. The first legal institutions were devised to regulate and ultimately to put an end to private war by requiring the vengeance of the injured kin to be bought off, and providing mechanical modes of trial in order to ascertain the facts. This idea of a regime of keeping the peace persists after many other functions have been added. It has but a limited field of social control for its province, leaving the greater part to the internal discipline of the kin group, the ethical custom of the community, and religious organization. But kin organization has substantially disappeared as a significant agency of social control. Organizations larger than the household exist today only for sentimental or historical or social purposes. Even the household has been losing its disciplinary effectiveness under the conditions of urban life. Juvenile Courts and Courts of Domestic Relations have taken over much of what was once the jurisdiction of the head of the family. A judge exercises authority to deal with truancy and incorrigibility, and proceedings in court replace the old-time interview between father and son in the family wood-shed which formerly taught the truant to fear God and his father and the policeman.

Religious organization was an effective agency of social control long after the kin group had ceased to be the social unit and even after politically organized society had attained not a little development. Often what we now call bodies of law in archaic societies were bodies of precepts declared by the priesthood and enforced by penances and exclusion from the society of the pious. In the beginnings of law much of this may be taken over by the state and given the sanction of force exercised by the officials of politically organized society. In England down to the Reformation and in parts of Continental Europe down to the era of the French Revolution, there was a system of church courts and church law which divided not unequally with the courts and law of the state the adjustment of relations and ordering of conduct. From the downfall of the Roman empire in the West to the twelfth century, the church bore the brunt of social control. From the beginning, the Christians were taught not to go to law with each other. They went with their controversies to the overseer of the local flock, the bishop, and he told them what the pious Christian would do in such a case. Out of this grew the bishop's court and a hierarchy of courts. Presently a body of law grew up for these courts, based on texts of Scripture, writings of the fathers of the church, canons of councils of the church, and decisions and rescripts of the popes, which has contributed much of the first significance to the law of today, and was in its time an agency of the highest importance toward maintaining and furthering civilization. But whatever hold religion may still have, religious organizations have lost their power over the mass of mankind. Social control has been all but completely secularized.

Morals have not had so effective an organization behind them. Yet the kin group disciplined the kinsman whose conduct brought reproach upon his kindred. At Rome, a power of censorship over morals, which first belonged to the king as patriarchal head of the Roman people, thought of as a society of kinsmen, passed to one of the magistrates of the republic and left remnants in the law which came down to the modern world. If such things no longer exist in politically organized society, trade and professional associations, trade-unions, social clubs, and fraternal organizations, with their codes of ethics, or their law or their standards of conduct or canons of what is done and what is not done, exercise, although in subordination to the law of the state, an increasing measure of control of individual conduct.

But since the sixteenth century political organization of society has become paramount. It has, or claims to have and on the whole maintains, a monopoly of force. All other agencies of social control are held to exercise disciplinary authority subject to the law and within bounds fixed by law. The English courts will restore to membership one who has been wrongfully expelled from a social club. Courts have decided whether property left in trust for church purposes was being used according to the tenets of the church for which it was given. The household, the church, the associations which serve to some extent to organize morals in contemporary society, all operate within legally prescribed limits and subject to the scrutiny of the courts. Today social control is primarily the function of the state and is exercised through law. Its ultimate effectiveness depends upon the application of force exercised by bodies and agencies and officials set up or chosen for that purpose. It operates chiefly through law, that is, through the systematic and orderly application of force by the appointed agents.

It would be a mistake, however, to assume that politically organized society and the law by which it brings pressure to bear upon individuals are self-sufficient for the task of social control in the complex society of the time. The law must function on a background of other less direct but no less important agencies, the home and home training, religion, and education. If these have done their work properly and well much that otherwise would fall to the law will have been done in advance. Antisocial conduct calling for regulation and ill-adjusted relations with neighbors will have been obviated by bringing up and training and teaching, leading to life measured by reason. But conditions of urban life and of industry have seriously affected home training. It is much less effective in the metropolitan city than it was in the small, homogeneous neighborhood of the past. The general secularization of things, and distrust of creeds and dogmas, and hard-boiled realism, as it likes to think itself, of the present time have loosened the hold of religion. Education has become our main reliance for the background of social control. That too, however, is secularized and has not found itself equal to training in morals, if indeed that can be achieved by teaching. The problem of enforcing its precepts has become acute as law takes the whole field of social control for its province.

Theories of what is have marked effect upon ideas of what ought to be. Men tend to do what they think they are doing. When the lawmaker is taught that law is the command of the sovereign, whose mouthpiece he is, he tends to think that the words "be it enacted" justify everything that he sets down after them. Arbitrary legislation excuses itself by saying such is the will of the sovereign. When the judge is taught that whatever the court decides is law because his decision gives what he decides the guinea stamp of the state, and that is all a legal precept requires, he is likely to think that the words "it is considered and adjudged" justify everything that follows them. When an administrative official is taught that law is whatever is done officially, he is likely to assume that he may refuse or neglect to hear both sides before making a determination, that he may act to receive complaints, to investigate, to prosecute, to advocate the complaint before himself, and to render judgment upon it in one proceeding, in violation of what had been taken to be a fundamental maxim of justice, that no one is to be judge in his own case. If lawmaker and judge and administrative official are taught that a law is a threat of exercise of the force of politically organized society they tend to leave out of account what is to be the content of the threat and consider only how far, in common speech, the threat can get by. Such ideas have come into vogue with the rise of absolute government throughout the world and give the autocrat the aid and comfort of scientific theory.

One of the leaders of juristic and political theory today, a zealous exponent of the doctrine that law is no more than a matter of authoritative laying down of norms by the appointed agency of a politically organized society and enforcement of threats that given a defined act or situation, neither qualified as good nor bad, certain legal coercion will follow—that leader among recent jurists tells us that idealism leads to autocracy and cites Plato in proof. The absolute ideal of the end of law and absolute measure of values seems to him to lead to absolute rulers setting up and maintaining them.

It is a paradox, no doubt, but so it is: absolute ideas of justice have made for free government, and skeptical ideas of justice have gone with autocracy. Idealism puts something above the ruler or the ruling body; something by which to judge them and by which they are held to rule. If the idea is absolute, those who wield the force of politically organized society are not. Skeptical realism puts nothing above the ruler or ruling body. There is no measure by which to judge them; at least, nothing more than the subjective opinion of the individual, and we are taught that of necessity no two can have the same measure of values, or if they have, no one can prove his measure to be better than another's. Hence, as St. Paul put it, having not the law they are a law unto themselves. What they do is its own justification. It is this attitude on the part of rulers that marks an autocracy. The autocrat rules as Kipling's tramp opened the lodge—by the authority in him vested and his strong right arm. I do not intend to preach a philosophical gospel of idealism. But I do say that if the doctrines of skeptical realism are the fruits of Neo-Kantian relativism in jurisprudence and politics, in such practical subjects we must judge relativism by its fruits. The answer, however, seems to me to be that we must not take relativism absolutely. This I shall consider in my last chapter.

Can we recognize that in immediate fact relations are adjusted and conduct is ordered by the application of force by those who exercise the power of politically organized society and stop there? Can we say, in reality there is the force of politically organized society enforcing the threats made by the lawmaker, and all behind the exercise of that force and all behind the threats are pious wish or superstition or pretense? Those who have felt, as on the whole men have since the Sophists announced the skeptical realist position twenty-three centuries ago—those who have felt that we must find a better basis for law, that we must find something behind force, that force cannot be the ultimate reality in social control, have, it is true, been driven from one position to another, without, however, giving up the idea that there is something permanent, or at least relatively permanent, in the background. The scholastic jurist-theologians saw revealed and discovered truth behind the phenomena of government—truth revealed by the Scriptures and truth discovered by reason. The jurists of the seventeenth and eighteenth centuries saw reason behind them. The metaphysical jurists of the nine-teenth century saw a metaphysically demon-strated unchallengeable fundamental from which law could be deduced. The historical jurists saw an idea of liberty realizing itself in human experience, and from that idea could deduce the legal system as the culmi-nation for the time being of the unfolding of that idea. Maine in Hegelian terminology put the abstract universal of the realizing of liberty as the concrete universal of progress from status to contract, and so putting the doctrine of Hegel and Savigny seemed to be moving toward positivism so as to lead some today to class him as a sociologist. The older positivism found laws of social development behind the evolution of politi-cally organized society and so behind the law through which it operates. A newer positivism, however, looks at the legal ordering of society to see what it is, not as all it can be and as giving us a measure of what ought to be, but as showing what measures have been used, and what urged, and how the law has been able to use them; to see what men have taken to be the end of law, and whether there is some idea behind what they have assumed and acted on which does serve to do what they are trying to do, namely, to maintain, further, and transmit civilization.

I can imagine someone saying to me that it is unscientific to criticize the theories of skeptical realism with reference to the results to which they lead in action. Certainly it would be futile to criticize theories of physical nature in this way. But we are not dealing with physical nature, as to which opinions of good and bad and criticisms of its phenomena are irrelevant. We are dealing with phenomena in the domain and under the control of the human will and what-is does not tell us the whole story. Here the ultimate question is always what ought to be. Unless governments exist for their own sake and judges and administrative officials judge and administer for the sake of exercising power, we cannot escape from the question: What is the end or purpose of the legal adjustment of relations and ordering of conduct? We cannot think of force as more than a means.

A rule of law without force behind it, says Jhering, is a contradiction in terms—"a

light that lights not, a fire that burns not."
Law involves force. Adjustment and ordering must rely ultimately on force even if
they are possible chiefly because of habits of
obedience on the part of all but an antisocial
residuum which must be coerced. Indeed,
the habit of obedience rests to no small
extent upon the consciousness of intelligent
persons that force will be applied to them if
they persistently adhere to the antisocial
residuum. The natural-law theory was not
wrong in opposing law to force, meaning
thereby force applied as such, upon no
principle, on subjective opinions of what
was expedient, or of the public good, or of
personal advantage of the individual func-
tionary. If it is not possible wholly to exclude
the subjective personal element in the
judicial and administrative processes, the
history of law shows we can go very far
toward doing it. Civilization rests upon the
putting down of arbitrary, wilful self-
assertion and the substitution of reason.
Even if we had not gone so far in achieving
this as we believed we had done in the last
century, one has only to compare the law of
the last century and the administration of

justice according to law in the last century
with that of colonial America to see how
much what we now think of as the com-
placent self-flattery of the nineteenth century was after all justified.

We have been told that the acid test of
theories of law is the attitude of the bad
man—the man who cares nothing about
justice or right or rights, but wants to know
what will happen to him if he does or fails
to do certain things. Is his attitude any more
a test than that of the normal man, who
objects to being subjected to the arbitrary
will of another but is content to live a life
measured by reason and takes part in the
choosing of those who are to exercise the
power of politically organized society in the
expectation and to the end that they exercise it, as the medieval lawyer put it, under
God and the law?

II

WHAT IS LAW?

"WHAT is truth,' said jesting Pilate, and would not stay for an answer." So wrote Bacon in his essay on truth. It was as natural for Bacon to assume that Pilate was jesting, when he read the fourth Gospel with sixteenth-century spectacles, as it was for Pilate to say what he said quite in earnest when he saw through first-century spectacles the saying of Jesus that he had come into the world to bear witness to the truth. Bacon knew that there had been philosophers who, as he put it, "counted it a bondage to fix a belief." But, he said, the philosophers of that sect were gone. They were, however, thoroughly in fashion in the first century, and any educated Roman of Pilate's time would have been likely to make the same remark to one who spoke with assurance about truth.

A radical change had taken place in thought between the classical Greek philosophy and the philosophy current at the end of the

Roman republic and the beginning of the empire, just as one had taken place between the beginning of the Christian era and the time when Bacon wrote, and again between Bacon's time and the advanced (as they consider themselves) thinkers of today.

Pilate spoke in an era of skepticism and disillusionment. The Peloponnesian War had exhausted the Greek city-states. All Greece had fallen into the hands of Philip and had been swallowed up in the empire of Alexander. That empire had fallen apart and was fought for by Alexander's generals and successors. The Hellenistic world was not one for idealist philosophies. The same may be said of Rome at the end of the republic and the beginning of the empire. The time was one of political breakdown and civil war. Three generations of civil war had exhausted the social organization of the time quite as the Peloponnesian War had exhausted the Greek world of the classical period. Disillusionment and unsettled conditions and autocratic governments had turned men to skepticism and Epicureanism, which seemed to tell men how to live in distracted times. These became prevailing types of thought and like the philosophies current today were philosophies of give-it-up. The Epicureans held that the only certain knowledge was that which we got through the senses. The highest good was the individual happy life. Justice was something variable and nothing more than an expedient toward happiness. The skeptics held that it was impossible for us to know anything about the nature of things and so the right attitude toward all things was one of imperturbability. Neither the senses nor reason could give us certain knowledge. We must suspend judgment about things and make the best of them. Only the skeptic who had suspended all judgment was able to look at things with an absolute calmness, unruffled by passion or desire. There was no possibility of positive judgments as to good or evil. If you saw bandits holding up a man, or a mob seeking to lynch an innocent man, Epicurus said get out of the way unless on a balance of pains and pleasures you could make out that interference would in the end promote your happy life. The skeptic said suspend judgment and hold off. The bandits or the lynching party are as likely to be right and as likely to be wrong as are you. Pilate spoke in that spirit.

Bacon wrote in the era of extravagant faith in reason that followed the Renaissance. The era of discovery and colonization and rise of great centralized political organizations, and of the beginnings of modern science and expansion of trade and commerce, was no time of disillusionment. Men were confidently assured that they could know all things and solve all problems through reason. Epicureans and skeptics were extravagant sects which had disappeared forever. Pilate's question was a bad jest.

In the present, after reason and faith in the possibility of knowledge attained through reason had ruled from Bacon's time to the end of the last century, we find ourselves in another era of disillusionment. The social philosophy of today gives up. Relativism teaches that all we can know is an individual mental creation made of our individual perceptions and experience. Our ideas of what ought to be are valid only in our individual systems of thought and cannot be proved to anyone else. There is an irrecon-

cilable antinomy between law and morals
and between social control by politically
organized society and justice. What-ought-
to-be is a pious wish, a superstition, an
unscientific, subjective picture unrelated to
reality. Judgments of good and bad, ascrib-
ings of praise and blame, are unscientific.
We postulate an ultimate political power
and all derives from it. Constitutional
limitations are contradictions in terms. A
pure science does not trouble itself about
subjective ideals of balance and guaranteed
liberties and rights. Rights are no more than
inferences from the exercise of the force
of politically organized society by state
officials. Law is no more than what those
officials do. Epicurus and Pyrrho and
Carneades have come back with new names
but with the same social, political, and
ethical philosophy.

Ever since the Greeks began to think
about such matters in the sixth century
before Christ, the question what is law has
been a battleground. Many things have
operated to make this a difficult question.
But not the least source of difficulty has been
that three quite different things have gone

by the name of law and men have tried to define all three in terms of some one of them.

Specifically the three meanings are: (1) What jurists now call the legal order—the regime of adjusting relations and ordering conduct by the systematic and orderly application of the force of a politically organized society. (2) The body of authoritative materials of or grounds of or guides to determination, whether judicial or administrative. This is what we mean when we speak of the law of Indiana or of comparative law or of the law of property or law of contract. (3) What Mr. Justice Cardozo has happily called the judicial process, to which today we must add the administrative process—the process of determining causes and controversies according to the authoritative guides in order to uphold the legal order. This is the meaning which many self-styled realists give to the term law today. As one of our well-known law teachers has put it, the law is whatever is done officially.

There are, then, these three ideas, and the three ideas each called by the one term have done much to confuse discussions of this subject. If the three meanings can be unified, it is by the idea of social control. We might think of a regime which is a highly specialized form of social control, carried on in accordance with a body of authoritative precepts, applied in a judicial and an administrative process.

Most of the controversy has raged about the nature of law in the second sense—the body of authoritative material of determination of controversies. But here also there is no simple conception. Law in that sense is made up of precepts, technique, and ideals: a body of authoritative precepts, developed and applied by an authoritative technique in the light of authoritative traditional ideals. When we think of law in the second sense we are likely to mean simply the body of precepts. But the technique of developing and applying the precepts, the art of the lawyer's craft, is quite as authoritative and no less important. Indeed, it is this technique element which serves to distinguish from each other the two great systems of law in the modern world.

For example, in the common law, the system of law of the English-speaking world, a statute furnishes a rule for the cases within its purview but not a basis for analogical reasoning. For that we look to experience of the administration of justice in the reported decisions of the courts. In the civil law, the system of the other half of the world which builds upon the Roman law, the technique in this respect is wholly different. The civilian reasons by analogy from legislative precepts and regards a fixed course of judicial decision on some point as establishing that precise point but not as providing a principle—an authoritative starting point for legal reasoning.

Again, there is the ideal element, the body of received, authoritative ideals. This element comes at bottom to the picture of the social order of the time and place, the legal tradition as to what that social order is and so as to what is the purpose of social control, which is the background of interpretation and application of legal precepts and is crucial in new cases in which it is necessary to choose from among equally authoritative starting points for legal reasoning.

Take, for example, a question in the law of torts upon which the English courts and many of our strongest American courts differ, on which, however, our American courts are not unequally divided, namely, the question of liability without regard to fault where something which one maintains upon his land, which is potentially liable to get out of hand and do damage, although not a nuisance, yet does escape and cause injury to a neighbor's land. Here we have to choose between the general security, calling for an absolute liability, and the individual life, calling for liability only where there has been fault. It has been suggested plausibly that the difference between the English conception of land as a permanent family acquisition and an American conception of land as an asset or a place to do things and carry on enterprises, in other words, a different ideal or picture of society, has dictated the starting points for reasoning.

Likewise, in interpretation the ideal element is decisive. Massachusetts and Missouri have differed in interpreting exactly the same language in statutes doing away with estates which descend to lineal heirs only by primogeniture. The language not being decisive, the question got down to one of the intrinsic merit of the possible interpretations. But how was that merit determined? Clearly by the ideal in the time and place of what an American social order should be. In New England the perpetuation of a family had a part in that picture which it did not have in the southwest.

The most familiar cases of the operation of the ideal element, however, are to be seen in the application of standards. Many standards involve an idea of reasonableness. The law enjoins what is reasonable under the circumstances. But there is no authoritative legal precept telling us that this is reasonable and that is not. One does not require any protracted study of decisions of the last generation on due process of law to see that application of the standard of reasonableness was governed by a received picture of a pioneer, rural, agricultural society, and that a picture of the urban, industrial society of today has been yielding different results.

Nor have we done with the complexities of the subject when we have distinguished the three meanings of law and the three elements in law in the second sense. For the precept element, which is commonly taken for all that we have to consider, is made up of rules, principles, precepts describing conceptions, and precepts prescribing standards.

A rule is a precept attaching a definite detailed consequence to a definite detailed state of facts. It is the earliest type of legal precept, and primitive law never gets any further. Primitive codes are made up of such precepts. For example:

In the Code of Hammurabi: "If a free man strike a free man, he shall pay ten shekels of silver."

In the Salic law: "If anyone shall have called another 'fox' he shall be condemned to three shillings."

In the Roman XII Tables: "If the father sell the son three times, let the son be free from the father."

Criminal codes are made up in greatest part of precepts of this sort.

A principle is an authoritative starting point for legal reasoning. Principles are the work of lawyers, organizing judicial experience by differentiating cases and putting a principle behind the difference, and by comparing a long-developed experience of decision in some field, referring some cases to one general starting point for reasoning and yet others to some other such starting point, or finding a more inclusive starting point for a whole field.

Consider such principles as that where one does something which on its face is an injury to another he must respond for the resulting injury unless he can justify it, or that one who culpably causes loss to another will be held liable for the injury, or that one person is not to be unjustly enriched at the expense of another. In none of these is there any definite detailed state of facts presupposed, and no definite detailed legal consequence is attached. Yet we continually turn to such principles as starting points for reasoning.

Or consider how starting from a principle as to the duty of a common carrier the precepts worked out for the carter were extended in one line to the stage coach, to the railroad, to the trolley line, to the auto-truck, to the airplane, without calling for new rules as one type of carrier succeeded another. Consider how in another line they were extended to telegraph, telephone, radio, gas, electric light, and power. Then note how lawyers worked out a broader principle as to duties involved in a public service, which has enabled our law to deal with one after another of these rapidly developing agencies of public service by affording a starting point for reasoning.

A conception is an authoritative category into which cases may be fitted so that, when placed in the proper pigeonhole, a series of rules and principles and standards becomes applicable. Examples are sale, trust, bailment. In those cases there is no definite detailed legal consequence attached to a definite detailed state of facts. Nor is there a starting point for reasoning. There are instead defined categories into which cases may be put, with the result that rules and standards become applicable—defined even if the definitions have to be revised from time to time and have to be much more elastic than rules.

Principles and conceptions make it possible to get along with many fewer rules and to deal with assurance with new cases for which no rules are at hand.

A standard is a measure of conduct prescribed by law from which one departs at his peril of answering for resulting damage or of legal invalidity of what he does. Examples are: The standard of due care not to subject others to unreasonable risk of injury; the standard of reasonable service, reasonable facilities, reasonable rates imposed upon public utilities; the standard of fair conduct of a fiduciary. Note the element of fairness or reasonableness in standards. This is a source of difficulty. As has been said, there is no precept defining what is reasonable and it would not be reasonable to attempt to formulate one. In the end, reasonableness has to be referred to conformity to the authoritative ideal.

Conduct requires standards. It is enough to remind you of one attempt to reduce conduct to rule, the old "stop, look, and listen" rule. Compare applying this rule to a horse and buggy, crossing a single-track railroad where trains ran thirty miles an hour, with a heavy motor truck crossing a four-line track on which streamlined trains as like as not go one hundred miles an hour. By the time the driver has stopped, got off the truck, looked up and down the tracks, got back on his truck and started up again, the streamlined train may have come four miles. A rule here will not do the work of the law. We are compelled to use a standard.

Two other theories of law from a different standpoint require notice. Many today say that law is power, where we used to think of it as a restraint upon power. Social control requires power—power to influence the behavior of men through the pressure of their fellow men. The legal order as a highly specialized form of social control rests upon the power or force of politically organized society. But so far from the law being power, it is something that organizes and systematizes the exercise of power and makes power effective toward the maintaining and furthering of civilization. What the power theory may mean in action has been exemplified in recent times in the identification of international law with power which has been leading to its undoing.

Another theory of today thinks of a law as an authoritative canon of value. Those who say this conceive that it is impossible to prove any moral principles or criteria of ought or measure of valuing conflicting or overlapping human demands. Hence those who wield the force of politically organized society, formulating the self-interest of a socially or economically dominant class, arbitrarily lay down or establish canons of value and constrain the rest of humanity to follow them. Well, I suppose socially and economically dominant classes have changed, and their self-interest has changed many times since Rome of the first and second centuries. But consider how many precepts formulated by the jurisconsults of that time have governed important relations and ruled important types of conduct ever since.

We must ever bear in mind that in law we have a taught tradition of experience developed by reason and reason tested by experience. One of the significant phenomena in the history of civilization is the vitality of such taught traditions. The civil law is a taught tradition of the universities from the fifth century to the present and connects with an older taught tradition of the schools of jurisconsults. The common law grew up as a taught tradition in the Inns of Court on the basis of the tradition of the courts. It was a taught tradition handed down from lawyer to apprentice from the seventeenth century and is now coming to be a taught tradition of academic law schools. Both of the two great legal systems of the modern world are taught traditions and so have proved resistant to forces that destroy political institutions. We have in our law such a tradition molded through the technique of the lawyer to the ever-changing circumstances of time and place and so one of the most enduring of human institutions. The last of the Caesars fell two decades or more ago. The work of the jurisconsults, contemporaries of the first Caesar, still guides the administration of justice in half of the world.

What is the source of authority of the legal order? When we ask this much-debated question we may mean the immediate practical source or the ultimate practical source or the ultimate moral source. Hence we cannot give one answer to a question which, seemingly simple, contains at least three questions, each with a different answer. The immediate practical source is to be found in the lawmaking and law-administering organs of a politically organized society, and behind them, as has been said, is the force of that society. So say the jurists. The ultimate practical source is a question for the science of politics. In our classical political theory we have been taught that it is consent; the consent of a free people to be ruled by a constitution and under it by laws made by legislators and administered by officials whom the people have freely chosen. Austin and Maine taught that it is a habit of obedience on the part of people generally, a phase, perhaps, of that control over internal nature which is half of civilization, making it unnecessary to apply force except in a relatively small number of the controversies which arise in daily life and to the conduct of a relatively small proportion of the population. Then there are those in recent times who tell us it is the self-interest of the dominant social and economic class. That class, we are told, imposes its will upon those who are not in a position or are too weak or too economically dependent to resist, and thus there arises the habit of obedience. When we come to the third question, we are in the domain of political ethics and political and legal philosophy.

But there are those who tell us that the question is superfluous. It is not a question of ought to be at all. In the ideal society of the future there will be no law since there will be no classes seeking one to impose its will upon others. With the disappearance of property, classes will disappear and law with them. Thus all question of ought is eliminated. Law has binding force because or when it is backed by a force imposing itself on all other forces. The classical juristic theory is that law may be deduced directly from justice, from the ideal relation between men, and owes its binding force to the binding force of justice which it declares. The dominant legal philosophy of today tells us that we cannot answer this question. As between the force theory and the consent theory and the justice theory, an assured choice is impossible. They express elements in the law which are in an irreducible antinomy, an ineradicable contradiction.

But the legal order goes on, whatever may be the basis of whatever rightful authority it has, and I submit it has kept and holds an actual authority because it performs, and performs well, its task of reconciling and harmonizing conflicting and overlapping human demands and so maintains a social order in which we may maintain and further civilization. So long as it does this well there will be the habit of obedience that makes practicable the employment of force upon those who require it.

When we have got so far we must pause to inquire how far, after all, the law in any of its senses can achieve this purpose. We must ask how far social control through politically organized society, operating in an orderly and systematic way by a judicial and administrative process applying authoritative grounds of or guides to decision by an authoritative technique, can stand by itself as self-sufficient and equal by itself to the maintaining and furthering of civilization. Thus we are brought to consider the limits of effective legal action, the practical limitations which preclude our doing by means of law everything which ethical considerations or social ideals move us to attempt.

One set of these limitations grows out of the difficulties involved in ascertainment of the facts to which legal precepts are to be applied. This is one of the oldest and most stubborn problems of the administration of justice. The legal precept assumes the facts as given us and on the given facts declares the appointed legal result. But the facts are not given us. It is a difficult process, beset with many chances of error, to ascertain them. Mistaken identity has led. to many miscarriages of justice. The necessity of rules and forms as to how things are to be done in order to prevent fraud and imposture sacrifices more than one meritorious case to the exigencies of the general security. Bentham said that portraits of Ananias and Sapphira ought to be hung in every court-room. But all the devices to which we resort in order to prevent perjury do not enable us to act with assurance on the testimony of witnesses on which we must mainly rely for giving us the facts.

A second set of limitations grows out of the intangibleness of many duties which morally are of great moment but defy legal enforcement. The story of the English schoolmaster who said, "Boys, be pure in heart or I'll flog you," has point for us. When the Roman law sought to make gratitude a legal duty and when our own law sought to hold promoters and directors of corporations to a high standard of disinterested benevolence, they succeeded no better than did the schoolmaster.

A third set of limitations grows out of the subtlety of modes of seriously infringing important interests which the law would be glad to secure effectively if it might. Thus grave infringements of individual interests in the domestic relations by tale-bearing or intrigue are often too intangible to be reached by legal machinery. Our law has struggled hard with this difficulty. But the results of our action on the case for alienation of affections, which long ago excited the ridicule of Thackeray, do not inspire confidence nor does the chief American precedent for enjoining a defendant from flirting with the plaintiff's wife assure a better remedy. So also with the so-called right of privacy. The difficulties involved in tracing injuries to their source and in fitting cause to effect compel some sacrifice of the interests of the retiring and the sensitive.

A fourth set of limitations grows out of the inapplicability of the legal machinery of rule and remedy to many phases of human conduct, to many important human relations, and to some serious wrongs. One example may be seen in the duty of husband and wife to live together and the claim of each to the society and affection of the other. Formerly, so far as the husband was concerned, our legal system secured this interest in three ways, namely, by a marital privilege of restraint and correction, by a suit for restitution of conjugal rights, and by a writ of habeas corpus directed to one who harbored the wife apart from her husband. But the privilege of restraint and correction is incompatible with the individual interests of personality of the wife and is no longer recognized. The suit for restitution of conjugal rights, in origin an ecclesiastical institution for the correction of morals, sanctioned by excommunication, has long been practically inefficacious and is now obsolete. And the writ of habeas corpus may now be used only when the wife is detained from the husband against her will. Today this interest has no sanction beyond morals and the opinion of the community. So little has been achieved in practice by the husband's actions against third parties who infringe this interest, tested in the law by centuries of experience, that the courts have instinctively proceeded with caution in giving them to the wife by analogy in order to make the law logically complete, and just as we had begun to give them to the wife many of our states found it necessary to take them away from both.

Law secures interests by punishment, by prevention, by specific redress, and by substitutional redress; and the wit of man has discovered no further possibilities of judicial action. But punishment has of necessity a very limited field and today is found applicable only to enforce absolute duties imposed to secure general social interests. The scope of preventive relief is necessarily narrow. In the case of injuries to reputation, injuries to the feelings and sensibilities—to the "peace and comfort of one's thoughts and emotions"—the wrong is ordinarily complete before any preventive remedy may be invoked, even if other difficulties were not involved. Specific redress is only possible in case of possessory rights and of certain acts involving purely economic advantages. A court can repossess a plaintiff of a tract of land, but it cannot repossess him of his reputation. It can make a defendant restore a unique chattel but it cannot compel him to restore the alienated affections of a wife. It can constrain a defendant to perform a contract to convey land but it cannot constrain him to restore the peace of mind of one whose privacy has been grossly invaded. Hence in the great majority of cases redress by way of money damages is the only resource and this has been the staple remedy of the law at all times. But this remedy is palpably inadequate except where interests of substance are involved. The value of a chattel, the value of a commercial contract, the value of use and occupation of land—such things may be measured in money. On the other hand, attempt to reach a definite measure of actual money compensation for a broken limb is at least difficult; and valuation of the feelings, the honor, the dignity of an injured person is downright impossible. We try to hide the difficulty by treating the individual honor, dignity, character, and reputation, for purposes of the law of defamation, as assets, and Kipling has told us what the Oriental thinks of the result. "Is a man sad? Give him money, say the Sahibs. Is he dishonored? Give him money, say the Sahibs. Hath he a wrong upon his head? Give him money, say the Sahibs." It is obvious that the Oriental's point is well taken. But it is not so obvious what else the law may do. If, therefore, the law secures property and contract more elaborately and more adequately than it secures personality, it is not because the law rates the latter less highly than the former, but because legal machinery is intrinsically well adapted to securing the one and intrinsically ill adapted to securing the other.

Finally, a fifth set of limitations grows out of the necessity of appealing to individuals to set the law in motion. All legal systems labor under this necessity. But it puts a special burden upon legal administration of justice in an Anglo-American democracy. For our whole traditional polity depends on individual initiative to secure legal redress and enforce legal rules. It is true, the ultraindividualism of the common law in this connection has broken down.

We no longer rely wholly upon individual prosecutors to bring criminals to justice. We no longer rely upon private actions for damages to hold public service companies to their duties or to save us from adulterated food. Yet the possibilities of administrative enforcement of law are limited also, even if there were not grave objections to a general regime of administrative enforcement. For laws will not enforce themselves. Human beings must execute them, and there must be some motive setting the individual in motion to do this above and beyond the abstract content of the rule and its conformity to an ideal justice or an ideal of social interest. The Puritan conceived of laws simply as guides to the individual conscience. The individual will was not to be coerced. Every man's conscience was to be the ultimate arbiter of what was right and wrong at the crisis of action. But as all men's consciences were not enlightened, laws were proper to set men to thinking, to declare to them what their fellows thought on this point and that, and to afford guides to those whose consciences did not speak with assurance. Such a conception, suitable enough in a sparsely settled community of pioneers, is quite impossible in the crowded industrial community of today with its complex organization and clash of conflicting interests. Yet many still think of law after the Puritan fashion. One social reformer told us recently that the real function of law is to register the protest of society against wrong. Well, protests of society against wrong are no mean thing. But one may feel that a prophet rather than a lawmaker is the proper mouthpiece for the purpose.

Those who believe in an omnicompetent state must postulate not Plato's philosopher kings but supermen administrators under a super-superman or a society in which supermen are in the majority, so organized as to commit the exercise of its powers to supermen. In the sublunary world in which we live law, if today the paramount agency of social control, needs the backing of religion and morals and education, even the more if it can no longer have the backing of organized religion and of the home.

III

THE TASK OF LAW

TO understand the task of the legal order consider the queue before the ticket window of a theater on the first showing of a new and well-advertised picture starring some popular favorite. Very likely many more are seeking admission than the theater can accommodate. If those seeking admission did not line up or were not lined up in this way, it might not be possible for many or even for any to get in. At any rate, the process of getting in would be a long and painful one in which many would be likely to be injured. Many would give up. Many others would be deterred by the scramble, would not try to join in it, and would turn about and go elsewhere. Very likely when it was over not only would few have succeeded in getting in out of many who essayed to, but they, with clothes torn, bruised, and battered, would be in poor condition to enjoy the performance. Or, compare the rush to get out of a burning building. If this is not ordered, few escape and many are trampled. But by ordering the buying of tickets or the exit from the burning building as many are served or saved as may be with the least friction and waste.

This ordering may result from customary recognition that lining up and taking one's turn is the thing to do or it may be constrained by a policeman or a teacher in a fire at a school. In either event social control makes it possible to do the most that can be done for the most people. As the saying is, we all want the earth. We all have a multiplicity of desires and demands which we seek to satisfy. There are very many of us but there is only one earth. The desires of each continually conflict with or overlap those of his neighbors. So there is, as one might say, a great task of social engineering. There is a task of making the goods of existence, the means of satisfying the demands and desires of men living together in a politically organized society, if they cannot satisfy all the claims that men make upon them, at least go round as far as possible. This is what we mean when we say that the end of law is justice. We do not mean justice as an individual virtue. We do not mean justice as the ideal relation among men. We mean a regime. We mean such an adjustment of relations and ordering of conduct as will make the goods of existence, the means of satisfying human claims to have things and do things, go round as far as possible with the least friction and waste.

In this way of looking at the matter, the point from which we must start is the claim or want or demand of the individual human being to have something or do something, or, it may be, not to be coerced into doing what he does not want to do. In the science of law these claims or demands or desires, since Jhering, have gone by the name of interests.

A legal system attains the end of the legal order, or at any rate strives to do so, by recognizing certain of these interests, by defining the limits within which those interests shall be recognized and given effect through legal precepts developed and applied by the judicial (and today the administrative) process according to an authoritative technique, and by endeavoring to secure the interests so recognized within defined limits.

I should define an interest, for the present purpose, as a demand or desire which human beings, either individually or through groups or associations or in relations, seek to satisfy; of which, therefore, the ordering of human relations and of human behavior must take account. The legal order or the law, in the sense of the body of authoritative guides to or grounds of determination of controversies, do not create these interests. There is so much truth in the old idea of a state of nature and theory of natural rights. Interests in this sense would exist if there were no legal order and no body of authoritative guides to conduct or decision. Claims of human beings to have things and do things have existed wherever a plurality of human beings have come into contact. There has never been a society in which there has been such a surplus of the means of satisfying these claims, or of room for everyone to do all that he sought and urged a claim to do, that there has not been competition to satisfy them. Conflicts or competition between interests arise because of the competition of individuals with each other, the competition of groups or associations or societies of men with each other, and the competition of individuals with such groups or associations or societies in the endeavor to satisfy human claims and wants and desires.

It is true the skeptical realists dissent from this proposition. They say the claims men make are a consequence of the law, not a cause of it. They tell us we do not secure my desire to hold my watch and use it exclusively because I claim it since my mother gave it to me, and my claim is recognized by politically organized society and given effect by a legally sanctioned right. They urge that I claim it because the law has taught me and others to claim things as owners. Having been thus taught to claim things, we work out a justification by attributing a right to ourselves—an antecedent moral claim—which we then say is backed by the state; whereas, it is said, if the law did not assign control to us we should not be claiming them. Let us see. Did workingmen strenuously claim a vested right in the job before or after recent legislation recognized and gave effect to it? Did the law teach workers to claim to conduct a sit-down strike or did they make the claim before the law ever heard of such a thing and have to be taught by the law that the claim could not be allowed?

We must begin, then, with the proposition that the law does not create these interests. It finds them pressing for security. It classifies them and recognizes a larger or smaller number. It fixes the limits within which it endeavors to secure the interests so selected, in view of other interests which are also recognized and in view of the possibility of securing them effectively through the judicial or administrative processes. It works out the means by which the interests may be secured when recognized and delimited. It prescribes canons of value for determining what interests to recognize, for fixing the limits of securing recognized interests, and for judging of the weight to be accorded in any given case to the practical limitations on effective legal action.

Interests, that is, the claims or demands or desires for which or about which the law has to make some provision if civilization is to be maintained and furthered, are asserted by individual human beings. But they are not for that reason all of them individual interests. We must not confuse interest as claim, as jurists use the term, with interest as advantage, as economists use it. Thinking of the claims or demands men make, interests fall into three classes, individual interests, public interests, and social interests. Some are claims or demands or desires involved immediately in the individual life and asserted in title of that life. These may be called individual interests. Others are claims or demands or desires involved in life in a politically organized society and asserted in title of that organization. Others, or some of the same in other aspects, are claims or demands or desires involved in social life in civilized society and asserted in title of that life.

Every claim does not necessarily go once and for all in one of these categories. The same claim may be asserted in different titles and may have to be looked at from different standpoints. It may be asserted in title of more than one aspect of life. Thus my claim to my watch may be asserted as an individual interest of substance when I sue someone who walks off with it without my consent, either to recover possession of it or to obtain its money value as damages for depriving me of it. But my claim may be looked at also as coincident with a social interest in the security of acquisitions and may be asserted as such when I by making due complaint procure the district attorney to prosecute for larceny someone who has stolen it from me.

It will be enough to give a general sketch of the scheme of interests which have pressed for recognition and security in the past. Individual interests may be classified as interests of personality, interests in domestic relations, and interests of substance. Interests of personality are those involved in the individual physical and spiritual existence. One form is the interest in security of one's physical person and bodily health. Another is in free exertion of one's will—freedom from coercion and from deception whereby one is led to do by force or trickery what he would not do freely or with knowledge of the facts. Another is in free choice of location, the claim to choose where he will go and where he will stay. Another is to one's reputation, to be secure against defamation and other aggressions upon his standing among his neighbors. Another is in free contract and freely entering into relations with others and, a closely related interest, in freely employing himself or gaining employment in any occupation for which he is or is thought to be qualified. Still another is in free belief and opinion. But each of these comes into competition with other· recognized interests and requires limitation. Thus, for example, the interests in freedom of contract and freedom to follow an occupation come into competition with claims of laborers, asserted through trade-unions, and have raised typically difficult questions for the courts and for legislation for more than a generation.

Individual interests in the domestic relations make many difficult problems. Husband and wife have each a claim or demand which they assert against the whole world that outsiders shall not interfere with the relation. Yet such abuses have proved to go along with the actions by which these claims were vindicated, that on a weighing of all the interests involved many states have been led to abrogate those actions. The interest is still recognized, but effective security is now denied it. Also the relation involves reciprocal claims or demands which husband and wife assert against each other. The claims of the husband to the society of the wife and to her services for the benefit of the household, which were formerly well secured, have come to be deprived of all substantial legal security on a weighing in comparison with the individual interest of the wife in individual free self-assertion. On the other hand, the claim or demand of the wife for support and maintenance by the husband is not only recognized but is provided for in a variety of ways which make it one of the best secured interests known to the law. As to the interests involved in the relation of parent and child, formerly the claims of the parent were given effect by privilege of "correction" (i.e., corporal punishment), by control of the child's earnings, and by a wide authority of shaping the training and bringing up of the child in every phase. But everywhere today individual interests of the child and a social interest in dependents have been weighed against the claims of parents; and juvenile courts, courts of domestic relations, and family courts in our large cities have greatly changed the legal balance of these interests.

Those claims or demands which are asserted by individuals in title of the individual economic existence are called interests of substance. You will think at once of claims to control corporeal things, the subject of the law of property; and of claims to the fulfilment of promised advantages, the subject of the law of contracts. But let us look instead at a group of interests in economically advantageous relations with others. Such relations may be social or domestic or official or contractual. If a man is wrongfully and maliciously expelled from a social club the injury to his reputation and his social standing in the community may have a serious economic effect upon him. Yet other claims must be thought of. The claims of other members to free determination of their own associations cannot be ignored. They cannot be compelled to associate with him as a fellow clubman if they persist in refusing to do so. In one case where a court ordered a wrongfully expelled mem-

ber restored to membership, the club rein-
stated him and then dissolved and formed a
new club, leaving him out.

I have already pointed out how claims of
the husband to the society and affection of
the wife and to her services for the benefit
of the household have ceased to be effectively secured either against outside interference with the relation or the wife's
refusal to adhere to it. Other interests have
come to be recognized and be conceded a
higher value. As to official relations, public
interests have to be weighed and the older
conception of property in a profitable office
has been given up. But the most significant
questions for our purpose have arisen with
respect to contractual relations. If one has a
contract with another, he makes a claim
against the whole world that third persons
shall not interfere to induce the other to
break the contract. Yet the third person may
assert claims which must be taken account
of in this connection. In the immediate past
some of the hardest questions in labor law
have turned on recognition of claims of
labor organizations to induce breaking of
contracts of employment and what should be

regarded as giving a privilege to interfere with such contracts.

Turning to public interests, one example of difficult questions of weighing will suffice. When political organization of society was struggling with kin organization and later with religious organization for the primacy in social control, the dignity of the state was a very serious matter. Recognizing this interest, it became settled that the state could not be sued without its consent, that its debts could not be set off against its claims, that it was not estopped by what was done by its officials, and that its claims were not lost by official neglect to assert them nor barred by limitation. There were other bases for some of these propositions. An interest in unimpaired efficiency of the political organization was also put in the scale. But now we are asking how far the dignity of the political organization of society is an interest entitled to weight. The extent to which the foregoing propositions should be maintained today, in view of changed ideas as to the dignity of the state, is a controversial subject in public law.

A whole lecture might be given up to a

catalogue of social interests. The one which has seemed most obvious in the past is the general security. This includes claims to peace and order, the first social interest to get legal recognition, the general safety, long recognized in the maxim that the public safety is the highest law, the general health, the security of acquisitions, and the security of transactions. One example of conflict or overlapping of recognized interests must suffice here. From the standpoint of the security of acquisitions one who wrongfully takes and holds another's property should not be able to transfer to a third person a better title than he has. But from the standpoint of the security of transactions, people generally who have no knowledge or notice of the owner's claim and, acting in good faith, part with value in a business transaction with one in possession of the property ought to be protected. It is claimed that possession, even if wrongful, ought to give a power of entering into business transactions as to the thing possessed and apparently owned. This question as to the limits of what is called negotiability has been coming up all over the world and recent legislation has been giving greater weight to the security of transactions in comparison with the security of acquisitions.

Closely related and hardly less important is the social interest in the security of social institutions, domestic, religious, political, and economic. Vexed questions as to divorce legislation turn on the relative weight to be given to the individual claims of husband and wife or to the social interest in marriage as a social institution. Vexed questions as between legislation against sedition and judicial maintenance of guarantees of free speech turn on the relative weight to be given to individual interests in free belief and opinion, subsumed under a social interest in general progress and in the individual life, or the social interest in the security of social institutions. Recent legislation is full of examples of the necessity of reconciling the security of economic institutions with the individual life.

Some other important social interests, namely, in the general morals, in the use and conservation of social resources, and in general progress, social, political, economic, and cultural, can only be mentioned in passing. But finally, and by no means least, there is the social interest in the individual life—the claim or demand asserted in title of social life in civilized society that each individual be secure in his freedom, have secured to him opportunities, political, social, and economic, and be able to live at least a reasonably minimum human life in society. Here, too, all manner of overlappings and conflicts are continually encountered and have to be adjusted. It is enough to say that every item in the catalogue must be weighed with many others and that none can be admitted to its full extent without impairment of the catalogue as a whole.

Nor is the task of the law finally achieved as to any claim or demand when it has been denied recognition or has been recognized and delimited. There is a constant pressure to recognize claims which have not been admitted. There is a constant struggle to obtain a higher valuing of claims which have obtained recognition. For example, the case pressed upon the legal order by organized labor has not been that laborers in such organizations and labor organizations were not treated as other litigants and litigant organizations were but that they were so treated. They considered that their claims were entitled to a higher value than that accorded by legal formulas which put them on the same plane with individuals generally and treated their disputes as ordinary controversies about trespass, breach of contract, and interference with contracts and business relations. Moreover, there are claims and conflicts of claims which have given rise to standing puzzles of the law. In one notable case lawmakers and jurists have debated and exercised their ingenuity since the time of Cicero and the problem is no nearer to a wholly satisfactory solution than it was then.

It is clear, then, that when an inventory of the claims or demands pressing for recognition has been made, the next step is to recognize or partially recognize or refuse to recognize them and to fix the limits of those which are recognized. Conceivably this may be done arbitrarily. But arbitrary adjustments of interests do not maintain themselves. Men feel a double grievance when not only are their claims and demands denied but they are denied otherwise than on a basis of reason. Ultimately recognition or denial of recognition of interests and de-limitation of those recognized is done in accordance with an established measure of values—something which I shall discuss in the last chapter. Then comes the question how to secure the interests recognized and delimited, and this brings us to the much-vexed question of rights. We secure interests chiefly by attributing to the one who asserts them what we call legal rights.

What is a right? It is said that an Irish jury in a manslaughter prosecution sent in a communication to the trial judge asking whether a man who had a spot in his skull where it was no thicker than an eggshell did not have a right to get killed if he went to the pig fair. Here "right" meant reasonable expectation. Apart from philosophical or metaphysical ethical considerations, a person may have reasonable expectations based on experience, or on the presuppositions of civilized society, or on the moral sentiment of the community. Some one or all of these may be recognized and backed by the law whereby they become the more reasonable. We say that a natural or a moral right has been made also a legal right. But the expectation may arise simply and solely from the law, in which case we say there is a legal right only. It is seldom that a legal right is conferred consciously and intentionally otherwise than as a recognition of reasonable expectations, or what are believed to be reasonable expectations, expressing presuppositions of civilized life.

Let us note what some of these presuppositions or postulates are. The most universal and fundamental may be phrased thus: In civilized society men must be able to assume that others will commit no intentional aggressions upon them. Whatever experience might have taught the Irish jury to expect at the pig fair, experience has taught us in this part of the world that we may go to the county fair with a reasonable expectation of not being hit on the head with a shillalah. Mark Twain said that the Leatherstocking tales ought to be called the "broken twig" tales because at the crisis of the story someone always stepped on a broken twig and then the Iroquois were upon him. In civilized society of today one does not have to keep below the sky line or avoid stepping on broken twigs. He does not as in fifteenth-century Italy have to turn wide corners in the city streets to avoid a bravo waiting to kill him if he keeps close to the wall. Our everyday life presupposes freedom from intentional attack.

Again, it is a presupposition, a jural postulate of civilized society, that those who are carrying on some course of conduct will do so with due care not to cast an unreasonable risk of injury upon others. So we cross the street in a reasonable expectation that no one will be driving against the lights and run into us.

Again, the moral sentiment of the community as well as the exigencies of the economic order requires men to keep their promises. It is a jural postulate that men will make good the reasonable expectations which their promises or other conduct reasonably create. So in the morning you lend your neighbor a dime to pay his street-car fare in the reasonable expectation that he will pay it back when next you meet him. All of these reasonable expectations are recognized and backed by the law. So you have a legal right to the integrity of your physical person and to have back the dime. But this tells the story historically only. The law took over certain ideas from experience shaped into postulates of civilized life and gave them the stamp of legal rights. How much more of a story there is, is something which has been argued since it was first raised by Greek philosophers of social control.

It is true the Greek philosophers did not argue about rights. They argued about what is right or what is just. But the Romans put law, systematic application of the force of politically organized society, behind what was right or just, and this led to the idea of rights. Hence the Greeks were thinking of what is the crux of the matter, namely, what is right or just as between conflicting and overlapping human claims. We may feel that a claim is such that it ought to be recognized and secured by law and then call it a natural right. It may be recognized by the general moral sense of the community and have back of it moral public opinion. Then we call it a moral right. It may, whether or not it has anything else behind it, have the law back of it. Then we call it a legal right. The Greeks had no clear idea of a right. They spoke of justice, of what was right, applied to a particular case. They thought rather of an established or legally recognized moral duty.

Nor is there a clear differentiation or clear conception of a right in Roman law. The Latin word which we translate as "a right" gets no nearer to what we understand by that term than in four of the ten meanings in which *jus* is used in the Roman law books. The four nearest meanings are (1) legally backed customary or moral authority, such as the authority of the head of a household; (2) power, a legally backed customary or moral power, such as the power of the owner of a thing to sell it; (3) liberty, a rightful freedom legally recognized, such as exercise of one's natural faculty of building a house on his land, even if it is an ugly shack and outrages the aesthetic sensibilities of his neighbors; and (4) legal position, position in the legal order, as, e.g., the *jus Latii*, the legal position of one who was not a citizen but had a status of qualified citizenship.

In the later Middle Ages, Thomas Aquinas gives us a suggestion of a just claim as a distinct conception. But it is not till the sixteenth century that *jus* as "a right" is distinctly set off from *jus* as what is right and *jus* as law. In the seventeenth century comes the transition from natural law to natural rights, from an ideal system of ideal precepts obliging to what is right to the claims to have things and do things which the ideal man would make in an ideal state (state of nature) and would recognize in other men. The resulting theory of law as a means of securing men in their natural rights held the ground in the science of law for three centuries. But in the end the natural rights of man became as tyrannous as the divine right of kings.

Grotius thought of a right as a quality. It was a quality inherent in a man as a rational being; a moral quality by reason of which it was right and just that one have certain things or do certain things. Such was the legal and political doctrine of the eighteenth century. Such were the inalienable rights asserted in the Declaration of Independence. Hobbes and Spinoza defined a right in terms of liberty. It was a condition of freedom from interference. Mr. Justice Holmes so put it in his classical lectures on the Common Law. A right, he tells us, is "a permission to exercise certain natural powers." It will be noted that while Hobbes and Spinoza speak negatively of legal noninterference with man's natural freedom, Mr. Justice Holmes speaks positively of a permission by politically organized society to exercise natural faculties. All three have their eyes upon one of the ways in which the law secures recognized interests, namely, by a regime of hands off, by leaving a whole field of action unhampered by legal precepts, by allowing a general condition of nonrestraint of men's natural faculties in certain situations and on certain occasions. In Continental Europe in the last half of the nineteenth century it was usual to put the Roman view, what is right backed by law, in a modern form. It was said that what was right in general was made the right of a particular man through the law.

Jhering changed the whole theory of a right by calling attention to the interest behind it. He said that a right was an interest protected by law. All interests were not rights. Those which the law recognized and secured were rights. I make a claim to my watch. I demand to be allowed to hold and use and control it. The law, in the sense of the regime of social control through the force of politically organized society, protects me in that claim or demand. Hence, says Jhering, I have a legal right to it. It will have been seen that Grotius and the nineteenth-century metaphysical jurists emphasize the ethical element, the moral valuation of the interest as the reason of securing it. On the other hand, Hobbes and Spinoza and Holmes and Jhering emphasize the political element. Whether or not the interest has a moral value, the securing of it by politically organized society makes a legal right.

But a legal right is something much more complex than these definitions in terms of some one feature of the recognition and securing of interests by the legal order would lead one to suspect. There is no word in jurisprudence with such a multiplicity of meanings. As one might say, it deserves an eight-hour day and pay for overtime. As a noun, the word right has been used in six senses. First, it is used to mean interest, as in most discussions of natural rights. Here it may mean what a particular writer thinks or feels should be recognized and secured on ethical grounds, or it may mean the interest recognized, delimited, and secured. Thus the rights asserted in the Declaration of Independence and the rights guaranteed by the bills of rights, are claims or demands which it is conceived ought to be recognized and given effect by governments, and in a constitution administered as the supreme law of the land they become rights in Jhering's sense. But there is in Jhering's theory a confusion of the protected interest and the legal institution that serves to protect it.

Second, then, it is used to mean the legally recognized and delimited interest plus the legal apparatus by which it is secured. This may be called legal right in the wider sense. Third, it is used to mean a capacity of constraining another or all others to certain acts or forbearances through the force of politically organized society—one of the bits of apparatus by which recognized interests are secured. Such is my legal right of possessing my watch and having possession restored to me if taken from me; my right of excluding others from my house; my right of exacting performance from someone who has promised in the legally appointed way; my right to the integrity of my physical person. This might be called legal right in the narrower sense. Fourth, it is used to mean a capacity of creating, altering, or divesting legal rights in the narrower sense, and so of creating or altering duties. This is better called legal power. Examples are the power of a pledgee to sell the pledgor's property; the agent's power to transfer the principal's property or bind the principal by a contract or make him liable by a tort; the power of one who has transferred land by an unrecorded deed to defeat the title by conveyance to a purchaser for value without notice who first records. In the last case, be it noticed, exercise of the power is a legal wrong. The law gives effect to it in order to uphold the security of transactions. But one who so exercises the power is liable to the person whose title has been cut off for the loss so caused him. Fifth, it is used to mean certain conditions of legal hands off, as it might be put, of legal nonrestraint of natural capacities. There may be a general condition of hands off as to a whole field of activity. Here we speak of a liberty. Such is what is called the right to pursue a lawful calling; i.e., the law does not constrain one to follow some particular calling but leaves to him his natural freedom of choosing one for himself. Again, an owner has a liberty of using and of enjoying the fruits of his property. Within the limits within which his interest is recognized, he may use and enjoy in such way as he likes. Or, instead, there may be a special condition of hands off on particular occasions, that is, exemptions from liability on particular occasions for what otherwise would be wrongs. These are better called privileges. Examples are the so-called right of deviation, i.e., privilege of passing over adjoining land, doing no damage, when the highway is impossible; the so-called emergency privileges, such as tying up a boat to a dock during a storm or running to shelter across a neighbor's land when chased by a lunatic with a hatchet; the privilege of confidential communication of defamatory statements by one interested in making to one interested in receiving them. Finally, sixth, right is used in a purely ethical sense to mean what is just. In the languages of Continental Europe the word which we translate as "right" has the additional meaning of law.

Interest, interest plus the legal apparatus for securing it, legal right in the narrower sense, power, liberty, and privilege need to be distinguished in any careful thinking. Unhappily we have no one word to use for the second meaning, which is often very important. But it was not till the last third of the nineteenth century in Continental Europe and the present century in England and America that the distinctions came to be made. It is no wonder that our terminology is still defective.

We must remember that an interest may be secured by a power without a legal right in the narrower sense. For example, the interest of a wife in being supported is secured by a power to pledge the husband's credit for necessaries. Yet at common law she had no action against the husband. Or an interest may be secured at the same time in a number of different ways. Thus, the interest of an owner of land is secured by a legal right of possessing it, a legal right of excluding others from it, a legal power of disposing of it, a liberty of using it and enjoying its fruits, and a privilege of abating a nuisance maintained by his neighbor which threatens it.

But all this had no more than been worked out by analytical jurists than, under the influence of the skeptical modes of thought described in a former chapter, jurists began to deny that there were such things as rights or that the claims recognized and secured by the legal order had anything more behind them than the force brought to bear by those who wield the authority of politically organized society. Thus Duguit says: "The individual man has no rights nor has the collectivity rights." That is, he maintains there are no qualities of men or moral claims or recognized interests behind the capacities of exacting acts or forbearances to which the law gives effect. The law simply enforces what it determines to be social functions. Everyone has a certain function to perform in society. He cannot be allowed not to perform this function because, if he were, a prejudice to society would result.

So every act that he does contrary to the function is repressed and all that he does to carry it out is protected. But his claims or demands or desires are quite irrelevant. Nevertheless, claims and demands and desires are continually pressed upon legislatures and courts and administrative agencies by individuals who will not be satisfied till some sort of provision is made for them. What Duguit really gives us is a canon of values for use in determining the recognition and delimitation of interests.

Juristic followers of Marx hold that it is all a matter of the self-interest of a socially or economically dominant class. The law, representing and expressing that self-interest, teaches some of us to expect certain things which it will constrain others to recognize and submit to. Rights are means of giving effect to private property. They will disappear in the ideal propertyless and so classless society of the future since they depend upon the power of a dominant class to enforce its self-interest upon those it holds in subjection.

Another type of thinker, developing a new type of analytical jurisprudence, holds that wrong is the elementary concept, not right and duty. There isn't a wrong because there is a violation of a right. There isn't a duty as correlative to a right. There is a wrong because someone has done something to which a rule of law has threatened to attach a consequence of some exercise of state force. If that force is exercised at suit of some individual, he may draw from it an unwarranted inference that he has a right. But the law did not make the threat in order to secure his right. His right is deduced from the effect of the threat. As Mr. Justice Holmes put it, the legal conception is washed in cynical acid and all ethical element is eliminated.

What shall we say of this threat theory of law and consequent threat theory of what we had been calling rights? If I lend you money is there nothing to think of beyond a threat to send a sheriff or a constable with an execution to collect the debt and pay the money back to me if you don't? If you convert my watch is there nothing to think about but the threat that if you do a constable may go out with a writ of replevin and retake it and give it back to me? If you slander me is there nothing to think of but a threat that if you do a jury may give a verdict against you for damages? If you accept appointment under a deed of trust is there nothing to think about beyond a threat that a court of equity may hold you to a standard of fair conduct and make you account to the beneficiary for profits made at his expense? If in all such cases there was nothing to think about beyond the particular state of facts, there would have to be a special threat laid down for every special state of facts. But since the eighteenth century not the most detailed of codes has attempted anything of that sort. It is because there are understood and recognized and delimited interests behind the threats, if you choose to call them such, and because there are received ideals of what we seek to achieve by means of the threats that we are able to deal with assurance with the great majority of new states of fact as they arise without having to formulate and promulgate new detailed threats in advance for each of them. The threat theory is the result of thinking of a body of law in terms of codes, such as a penal code, conceived of as providing in advance a threat of a definite, detailed consequence for every definite, detailed state of facts.

This idea that there are no rights, that there are only threats announced by the ruling organ of a politically organized society, from which, if executed, individuals may obtain certain advantages, is a symptom of the rise of political absolutism all over the world. Under an absolute polity and under the reign of such juristic theories there is no need for the autocrat or the bureaucrat to be troubled about the rights, that is, the interests or claims or demands (whether rightful or moral or just or reconcilable with those urged by others) of anyone. Constitutional guarantees are guarantees of phantoms. They may be ignored. It is enough that the ruler has issued threats and has a strong political organization under his control to make them good. It is enough that an administrative official has been given power to execute certain threats. No one has any standing to set up rights against his manner of exercising that power. Such ideas on the part of administrative agencies, not at all uncommon in the government of the time, are the fruit of theories that we can't prove anything in the nature of a claim to be secured, that we can't establish with assurance any measure of values, that there is no way of reaching conviction that, on the one hand, claims which we recognize should be limited in view of other claims or, on the other hand, that one claim should be preferred to the other on the basis of ascribing to it values and weighing those values, and that there is nothing in law but an aggregate of threats. We cannot do better than we try to do. If we give up what we have sought to do in the past and say "let those who control the force of politically organized society make such threats as seem good to them, either upon such reasons as appeal to them or without reasons," we give up what has made law a prime agency of civilization since the days of the classical Roman jurists.

It is a boast rather than a description to call such teachings "realism." They ignore one of the most significant features of social control by politically organized society, namely, the attempt to carry it on upon a basis of reason and toward what is conceived of as justice. This so-called juristic realism is akin to artistic realism with its cult of the ugly and false dogma (for those who abhor dogma can be as dogmatic as those who preach it) that the ugly exists, therefore the ugly is significant. Features of the legal order have always existed and some now exist which depart from or fall short of our ideals which we seek to attain. Yet in the history of civilization, as our control over internal nature has advanced, we have been able more and more to control the departures and approach more nearly to the ideals. Which is the significant feature of the legal order on which to build juristic theory, the departures and fallings short or the increasing control of the departures and increasing reduction in the fallings short?

Let me illustrate by the example of artistic realism. Some time ago the friends of a law school presented to it a portrait of a judge, a graduate of the school, whose long career upon the bench had been one of exceptional devotion to the ideal of justice and outstanding achievement for the public welfare. The artist was eminent in his calling and has since been chosen to execute important projects at the national capital. But on this occasion, at least, he felt bound in the interests of truth to be a realist. It seems that the judge has a big fist and a habit of holding it before him when in thought. None of his friends had noticed this, but the artist saw it and saw in it the truth. So he put the great fist in the foreground as the outstanding feature of the portrait. There it stands out arresting the attention of the observer. If one's gaze can succeed in getting beyond the fist, he may see, not much emphasized, the thoughtful countenance of the judge. But for most observers the fist is the whole picture. It cuts off view of the countenance. Which, however, is the significant feature of the judge, the big fist (which certainly does exist) or the thoughtful face?

What is significant is the claim behind the legal right. Without a recognized claim, recognized on a basis of reason, there is only an arbitrary exercise of force for its own sake, something against which we rebelled at the Revolution and to prevent which we set up frames of government founded on a separation of powers with a bill of rights in the forefront of them on the very morrow of the Declaration of Independence.

What is called a threat, from the stand-point of the bad man made the test of juristic theory, may be otherwise described according to the standpoint from which it is looked at. From the standpoint of the individual at the crisis of action, we may call it a rule pointing out the right path to the conscientious good man who seeks to know where it is and to walk in it no less than the unconscientious man who would like to walk in a different one but fears to do so. From the standpoint of the judge at the crisis of decision, it is a rule or principle for his guidance prescribing or leading him to a just determination. From the standpoint of the counselor, who seeks to advise the bad man what he must look out for and the good man how to proceed in the appointed manner, it is the basis of prediction as to what course the officials, who wield the power of politically organized society, will take as to the enterprise he is conducting.

It is true that from each of these standpoints one may develop the idea of a law as a threat. But are we compelled to do so from any of them? If in order to be scientific and realist we must be hard-boiled, can we not insist on the claims or demands or desires, actually asserted, as our starting point and ask how we can make threats which will adjust them to each other and secure them within the limits consonant with securing other claims of other men? Is it not a real problem, something more than a pious wish, to find how to recognize the claims of A and those of B without destroying either—and without leaving it to A and B to seek a solution by trying each to destroy the other? When entrusted with power men will tend to be arbitrary. From the beginning, the law has sought to repress that tendency and, on the whole, has succeeded well in doing so. Let us not concede to the give-it-up philosophers that the tendency cannot be repressed and that those who wield the power of politically organized society are bound to be arbitrary whether they will or no. Such was not the philosophy which has been the creative force in legal history since the classical era of Roman law. Such was not the philosophy which made the writings of Roman jurists from Augustus to Alexander Severus a quarry for lawyers and lawmakers in every part of the world ever since. Such was not the philosophy of those who made the concrete provisions for redress of concrete grievances in Magna Carta into bills of rights which guarantee freedom throughout the English-speaking world. Such was not the philosophy which enabled us to make the English medieval land law and seventeenth-century procedure the basis of a law for nineteenth-century America. Such was not the philosophy which has made civilization and law go forward together since the revived study of Roman law in the twelfth century.

IV

THE PROBLEM OF VALUES

DIFFICULT as it may be, the problem of values is one from which the science of law cannot escape. Even the crudest or most blundering or most capricious adjustment of relations or ordering of conduct has behind it some canon of valuing conflicting and overlapping interests. It may be merely keeping the peace. It may be preserving the social *status quo*. It may be promoting a maximum of free individual self-assertion. It may be enforcing the self-interest of a dominant social or economic class or of one seeking to become dominant. It may be maintaining and furthering the power of an established political organization. If at times and in places such canons of value have been held more or less unconsciously, with the advent of lawgivers and lawyers they have increasingly been given systematic development and formulation and have been brought increasingly into relation with the postulates of life in civilized society. In the classical eras of legal history, both in the ancient and in the modern world, demonstration or criticism or logical application of such canons of value have been among the chief activities of jurists. The contact of Roman lawyers with Greek philosophy, the teaching of Roman law side by side with the teaching of theological ethics in medieval universities, the emancipation of jurisprudence from theology and of law from the text of Justinian with the coincident rise of philosophy of reason, and the rise of historical jurisprudence with coincident metaphysical theories of liberty, mark epochs in the science of law because in each case canons of value were adapted to the juristic tasks of the time and brought into accord with the social ideal of the time and place.

Jurists have conceived of a legal order patterned upon a divine order and so have turned to authority to provide a canon. They have thought of conformity to a moral order as revealed by the analogy of the order of physical nature, or as partly ascertained from revelation and partly discoverable by reason. At other times, they have conceived of the legal order as a rational order and so of a canon of values derived from pure reason. Reason, in this mode of thought, was taken to reveal a natural or ideal law of universal and unchallengeable validity, even if, as we see it now, an ideal version of the positive law and legal institutions of the time and place. At still other times they have thought of the legal order as resting upon experience, and so of a canon of values representing experience of life in civilized society. In that mode of thought, experience of life was conceived of as developed by experience in adjusting relations and ordering conduct through political and legal institutions, put into formulas by lawmakers and judges and doctrinal writers, and criticized and systematized by jurists. Thus they have conceived of the legal order as a historical order. At still other times, they have thought of the legal order as an order of freedom, as a regime of securing to everyone the maximum of free exertion of his will consonant with a like measure of free exertion of his will by everyone else. In this view there is a canon of values demonstrated by metaphysics. More recently there have been attempts to found a canon of values upon economics or to derive one from a theory of class war, attributing value to a class rather than to individuals and to claims urged in title of a class rather than in title of individual life or of social life, looking at society as a whole.

Where are we in juristic theory today? Some urge a maximum satisfaction of material wants. More argue that it is impossible to arrive at any measure of values or for judges and officials to hew to one if it is established. The former put this on epistemological grounds. The latter base the conclusion on Freudian psychology. Be the criterion of values in the books what it may, the actual behavior of judges and officials will be motivated by wish, and reason and authority will be conjured up afterward to satisfy another wish, namely, to appear reasonable. The former hold that a law is a threat of exercise of state force and so conceive of an order of force. The latter interpret judicial and administrative action in terms of individual psychology and so conceive of an order of impulse.

Mr. Justice Holmes, putting the matter, however, from the analytical standpoint as against the metaphysical jurisprudence of the last century, expressed himself more than once in what seems to reduce law in all its senses to force. For example: "It seems to me clear that the *ultima ratio* not only *regum* but of all private persons, is force." But this does not mean that force is the ultimate legal measure of values. It means that the measure of values, in order to be an effective measure, must in the end be backed by force. Again, he said a generation later: "When it comes to the development of a *corpus juris*, the ultimate question is what do the dominant forces of the community want and do they want it hard enough to disregard whatever inhibitions stand in the way?" Yet what the dominant forces of the community have wanted has in the past been put in an ideal form by jurists, and the legal measure of values has been found in conformity to that ideal rather than in concrete wants in each case as it arose. Today, on the other hand, the doctrine of each single decision or administrative determination, carrying out a threat or expressing a concrete wish in the case in hand, treated as unique, as being of itself the law, goes very much further than Mr. Justice Holmes toward putting the legal order as a simple order of force. He thought of morality as "a check on the ultimate domination of force." The founders of our polity thought of law as a check upon exercise of force by those who wielded the authority of politically organized society. The doctrine of the moment is that checks are illusion. The very existence of the force, when exerted by agents of a politically organized society, is law.

What such a doctrine may mean in practice is well shown by the present status of international law. As a theory of what has become the paramount agency of social control, it cannot be satisfying. It is no doubt true that we cannot demonstrate a measure of values as something everyone must accept and abide. But we are not bound for that reason to hold the legal order in abeyance until that impossible task has been achieved. Law is a practical matter. If we cannot establish a demonstrated universal legal measure of values which everyone will agree to, it does not follow that we must give up and turn society over to unchecked force. There have been centuries of experience of adjusting relations and ordering conduct by law, and we have learned to develop that experience and make use of it in weighing and valuing interests. Einstein has taught us that we live in a curved universe in which there are no straight lines or planes or right angles or perpendiculars. Yet we do not on this account give up surveying. Straight lines and planes and so forth do not exist. But as postulates of a practical activity they are near enough to the truth for the practical needs of a practical activity. So it is with the measure of values postulated or accepted in modern systems of law. If we cannot prove them, we can use them, as sufficiently near to the truth for our practical purposes.

How has the law gone about this matter of a measure of values in practice?

If we look at the actual working out, development, and application of legal precepts rather than at juristic theory, we may say that three methods have obtained. One is a finding out by experience of what will achieve an adjustment of conflicting and overlapping interests with the least impairment of the scheme of interests as a whole and giving that experience a reasoned development. Thus the measure becomes a practical one of what will adjust relations and order conduct with the least friction and waste. If we bear in mind that he uses "right" in the sense of legally recognized interest, this is well put by Dicey:

How can the right of combined action be curtailed without depriving individual liberty of half its value; how can it be left unrestricted without destroying either the liberty of individual citizens, or the power of the Government? To see that this problem at the present day presents itself everywhere, and has nowhere received a quite satisfactory solution, is of importance. The fact suggests at least two conclusions: The one is, that the difficulty felt in England in dealing with our combination law arises, to a great extent, neither from the greediness of employers nor from the unreasonableness of workmen, but from the nature of things; the other is, that the most which can be achieved by way of bringing into harmony two essentially conflicting rights, namely, the right to individual freedom and the right of association, is to effect a rough compromise between them. Such a practical solution of a theoretically unsolvable problem is sometimes possible. That this is so is proved by our existing law of libel. It is a rough compromise between the right of X to say or write what he chooses, and the right of A not to be injured in property or character by X's free utterance of his opinions. The compromise is successful; it substantially allows freedom of discussion, and at the same time protects Englishmen against defamation.[1]

It is in this way that the legal order actually functions. This is what courts do and judges and jurists have been doing at least since the Roman jurisconsults of the first century. In the whole development of modern law, courts and lawmakers and law teachers, very likely with no clear theory of what they were doing but guided by a clear instinct of practical purpose, have been at work finding practical adjustments and reconcilings and, if nothing more was possible, practical compromises, of conflicting and overlapping interests. Many of the adjustments worked out by Roman jurists in the first two and a half centuries of the Christian era have stood the test of time and have survived all manner of social and economic and political changes and obtain throughout the world today. There is at any

1. Dicey, *Law and Public Opinion in England during the Nineteenth Century*, p. 468. By permission of The Macmillan Company, publishers.

rate an engineering value in what serves to eliminate or to minimize friction and waste. William James held that there was an ethical value in what gives the most effect to human demand with the least sacrifice.[2] If one accepts the civilization interpretation of the Neo-Hegelians, he may hold that this adjustment of competing interests with a minimum of waste makes for civilization and so has a philosophical value.

But the practical process of the legal order does not stop at finding by experience —by trial and error and judicial inclusion and exclusion—what will serve to adjust conflicting or overlapping interests. Reason has its part as well as experience. Jurists work out the jural postulates, the presuppositions as to relations and conduct, of civilized society in the time and place, and arrive in this way at authoritative starting points for legal reasoning. Experience is developed by reason on this basis, and reason is tested by experience. Thus we get a second method, namely, valuing with reference to the jural postulates of civilization in the time and place. Newly arising

2. James, *The Will to Believe*, pp. 195–206.

claims are measured by these postulates when they push for recognition. When recognized they are adjusted to other recognized interests by this measure. When they are delimited with reference to other interests the means of securing them are determined by this same measure.

A generation ago I sought to formulate the jural postulates of civilized society in our time and place, for the purposes of systematic exposition of private law (i.e., the law governing individual interests and relations of individuals with their fellows) in five propositions, with certain corollaries. For the present purpose we need not look at the corollaries. What I sought to do was to formulate what was presupposed by the law as to possession, as to property, as to legal transactions and resulting relations, and as to wrongs. As I should put them now they read:

1. In civilized society men must be able to assume that others will commit no intentional aggressions upon them.

2. In civilized society men must be able to assume that they may control for beneficial purposes what they have discovered

and appropriated to their own use, what they have created by their own labor, and what they have acquired under the existing social and economic order.

3. In civilized society men must be able to assume that those with whom they deal in the general intercourse of society will act in good faith and hence

(a) will make good reasonable expectations which their promises or other conduct reasonably create;

(b) will carry out their undertakings according to the expectations which the moral sentiment of the community attaches thereto;

(c) will restore specifically or by equivalent what comes to them by mistake or unanticipated or not fully intended situation whereby they receive at another's expense what they could not reasonably have expected to receive under the circumstances.

4. In civilized society men must be able to assume that those who are engaged in some course of conduct will act with due care not to cast an unreasonable risk of injury upon others.

5. In civilized society men must be able to

assume that those who maintain things likely to get out of hand or to escape and do damage will restrain them or keep them within their proper bounds.

Professor Hocking considered that these postulates established "the liaison between philosophy and the science of law."[3] At any rate, they seemed to be borne out by the law as it stood at the end of the last century and to afford a measure of value for newly asserted claims. But it has been becoming more and more evident that the civilization of the time and place presupposes some further propositions which it is by no means easy to formulate, since the conflict of interests involved has by no means been so thoroughly adjusted that one may be reasonably assured of the basis upon which the adjustment logically proceeds.

In general, a postulated claim of the job holder to security in his job is becoming recognized. But exactly in what sort of job holders and in what sort of jobs a right is to be recognized is far from clear. Moreover, the regime of collective bargaining with

3. Hocking, *The Present Status of the Philosophy of Law and of Rights*, p. 95.

organizations commanding a majority of votes in a plant seems to involve a proposition that the minority are not to have a recognized right to their jobs as against the prevailing majority organization. The most that can be said at present is that the employer-employee relation is being removed from the domain of contract and is coming to involve a security of tenure not depending upon agreement.

Another emerging jural postulate appears to be that in the industrial society of today enterprises in which numbers of men are employed will bear the burden of what might be called the human wear and tear involved in their operation. Some such postulate is behind workmen's compensation laws. But in the administration of those laws there is much to suggest a wider proposition. There are also other indications of a third proposition, which may come to include the second, namely, that the risk of misfortune to individuals is to be borne by society as a whole. Some such postulate seems to be behind what has been called the insurance theory of liability and is behind much social security legislation. Perhaps a reaching out for something of the sort has been behind a tendency of juries to hold that, whenever anyone has been hurt, someone able to respond in damages ought to pay. In such cases Lord Bramwell used to tell the jury a story of the pickpocket who went to a charity sermon and was so moved by the preacher's eloquence that he picked the pockets of everyone within reach and put the contents in the plate. Or, again, he suggested that some would have a judge charge a jury in this fashion: "Gentlemen, the only question is which do you *really* feel sorry for, the plaintiff or the defendant?" Use of general verdicts to promote "an equitable division of the economic surplus," a well-known phenomenon, may have behind it some crude idea of distributing the burden of the risks involved in life in an industrial society. Certainly there were no such presuppositions of life in the last century. They seem to be more and more assumed in the society of today. What may be said with assurance is that the last century had a marked tendency to look at interests to the measure of the general security. Today there is a growing tendency to look at them to the measure of the individual human life. It is no wonder that the law on some subjects is coming to be more at large than is compatible with the exigencies of a well-conducted economic order.

A third measure of values, used in the classical era both in Roman law and in the law of the modern world, and well established in the maturity of law, is found in a received, traditionally authoritative idea of the social order and hence of the legal order, and of what legal institutions and doctrines should be and what the results of applying them to controversies should be.

It need scarcely be said that such pictures of an ideal social order, which come to enter into the law as part of the authoritative guides to determination of controversies, are not photographs or even idealized photographs of the social order of the time and place. They are instead much more idealized pictures of the social order of the past, undergoing a gradual process of retouching with reference to details of the social order of the present. Thus the received ideals of American law, as they took shape in our formative era in the fore part of the nineteenth century, are much closer to the pioneer agricultural society of our past than to the typically urban, industrial society of twentieth-century America. In general, men have sought to explain the institutions of the present in terms of a picture of the social order of the past.

For example, Plato's *Republic* is a picture of an ideal Greek city-state. Aristotle's *Politics* is a treatise on government in terms of the Greek city as an independent, politically and economically self-sufficient unit. Each had Sparta in mind when the Spartan type of state was passing from the stage. Each had in mind the Greek city-state when the days of such states were over. Again, the medieval jurists had before their minds the academic conception of the "empire"—the conception of an empire embracing all Christendom and continuous with that of Augustus and Constantine and Justinian. This idea of a universal empire with a universal law gave rise to an ideal which has been received in the law of half of the modern world and is still of cardinal significance in legal thinking everywhere. Yet it arose and was given shape when the Roman empire, of which it was an idealization, was utterly in the past and the world was on the eve of the nationalism which followed the Reformation.

Again, consider the picture behind our classical seventeenth-century law books, the received ideals of the social and legal orders as they appear in *Coke on Littleton* and Coke's *Second Institute*. In our formative period these books were oracles in the new world for our private law and public law respectively. Certainly, there was behind them no picture of colonial American society. Nor were they written on a background of Elizabethan society. The system described in Littleton's *Tenures* was moribund when the book was written. It is no more in the spirit of the England of Shakespeare than the pedantic formal logic of *Coke on Littleton* was anything but an anachronism in the days of Bacon. Yet this spirit of medieval England, this idealized picture of pre-Reformation England, was an enduring element in the body of legal materials which came to govern English-speaking peoples everywhere.

Again, international law furnishes an excellent example. Since the seventeenth century, international law has had for its background a picture of the political world as it was when Grotius wrote. The seventeenth and eighteenth centuries were an era of absolute governments. Personal sovereigns of the type of the king in the old regime in France ruled in the significant countries of western Europe. The problem of international law was one of adjusting the relations and guiding the international conduct of these personal sovereigns. They made war with highly trained regular armies. They represented their several countries so completely that for practical purposes international relations could be treated as relations between sovereigns, and the rules of war as limitations on the belligerent conduct of sovereigns. International law grew up to this picture and we still think and speak to its pattern. Yet it long ago ceased to portray reality.

One may tell the same story of the picture of the society ordered by law today to which, as the received ideal, the details of the administration of justice still tend to conform. It is one which has governed from the seventeenth to the nineteenth century, getting what is likely to prove its final form in the latter. It is a picture in which relation is ignored and each man is made to stand out by himself as an economically, politically, morally and hence legally self-sufficient unit. He is to find his place for himself by free competition. The highest good is the maximum of free self-assertion on the part of these units. The significant feature of these units is their natural rights, that is, qualities by virtue of which they ought to have certain things or be free to do certain things. The end of law is to secure these natural rights, to give the fullest and freest rein to the competitive acquisitory activities of these units, to order the competition with a minimum of interference. Only a decade ago one had outwardly to do lip service to this picture on pain of being branded socialist or communist. It could hold on longer with us than elsewhere because it did portray reasonably well a pioneer, rural, agricultural society in a land with a great unsettled public domain and natural resources awaiting exploitation. But it has ceased to be a true picture of the society in which the legal order must be carried on today.

No less than six important changes in juristic thought have taken place in the last fifty years—all tending in a new direction.

One is the insistence on function rather than on content; the tendency to ask how do precepts work, to ask whether they can be made to bring about just results rather than whether their abstract content is abstractly just. The moment we ask such questions, however, we are driven to inquire as to the end of law. For function means function toward some end. Thus for a generation philosophical discussion as to the end of the legal order has taken a continually larger place in jurisprudence.

Second, there has been a shift to an economic emphasis, putting the emphasis on wants rather than on wills, thinking of free self-assertion as but one of many human wants or demand or desires, and seeking a maximum satisfaction of wants rather than a maximum freedom of wills.

Third, there has come to be an objective, as contrasted with a subjective emphasis, as, for example, in the general giving up of Savigny's theory of contract, which the law teachers of the last century, particularly in

England, sought to fasten upon the common law. That theory flowed from the idea of the will as the central point in jurisprudence. Hence the general abandonment of it today is significant.

Fourth, we must remark the emphasis on concrete claims of concrete human beings instead of on the abstract will of the abstract individual. Many causes, social, economic, and political have contributed to require this shift of stress. What especially compelled jurists thereto was the development of psychology in the later part of the last century and in the present generation. Under attack from modern psychology, "the individual," in the sense of nineteenth-century metaphysical jurisprudence, and the "individual will," in the sense of the nineteenth-century pandectists and their English followers in analytical jurisprudence, were as insecure foundations as the "natural man" and the "state of nature" had proved to be under the attacks of the critical philosophy of a century before.

Fifth, we have to note the movement for teamwork with the other social sciences; the study of law as part of a whole process of social control. This is an essential point in the twentieth-century sociological jurisprudence. Compare it with the characteristic noncoöperation of the social sciences in the nineteenth century. This ignoring by each of the social sciences of each of the others was by no means wholly due to the exigencies of university organization and academic courtesy, requiring each scholar to keep off of his neighbor's premises. It was in the very spirit of the last century—every man for himself, every subject for itself. It was in the spirit of the atomistic conception of humanity as an aggregate of individuals engaged, with a minimum of organization, in a competitive acquisitive struggle for existence. Each subject was thought of as being as independent and self-sufficient as the independent and self-sufficient individual who pursued it.

Sixth, we must take note of the recognition of the problem of a measure or canon of values as something much wider than a problem of jurisprudence—as a problem of all the social sciences, to be looked at in jurisprudence both as such and in its special relation to all the mooted questions of the

science of law. This is something which
cannot be dodged by a "pure science of law"
which seeks to repeat the method of English
analytical jurisprudence and relegate it to
some other science. A jejune jurisprudence
which has cast out the ideal element of law
and all consideration of what the precepts of
what-ought-to-be ought to be simply invites
the bringing of that element and that consideration back in unconsciously by side
doors, and conscious or unconscious blundering, and the sort of judicial process which
the self-styled realist of the moment takes to
be significant.

Not yet one half of the present century
has elapsed. It is not until the second half of
a century that what prove to be its characteristic modes of thought stand out definitely.
The influence of the epoch-making writing
of Jhering in 1884 began to be felt generally
in America after half a century. Manifestly
one cannot speak with assurance as to how
we are in the end to value competing and
overlapping interests in the present century.
But some part of the path of the juristic
thought of tomorrow is already apparent. It
seems to be a path toward an ideal of co-

operation rather than one of competitive self-assertion. Yet coöperation cannot be a wholly satisfactory measure of values for a system of law. For coöperation is a process. It must be coöperation toward something. I suspect that the idea will prove to be co-operation toward civilization. But I cannot pretend that I can draw this from the actual phenomena of the legal order and the judicial process with the same assurance with which I can draw the ideal of free competitive individual self-assertion from the phenomena of the legal order and the judicial process and the juristic process (as one may well call it) in the nineteenth century.

Until recently a tradition, sometimes amounting to a settled habit of noncoöpera-tion, began in the locality at the bottom of the local administrative scale and extended to the top in the departments of the Federal Government. It was and still is to no small extent manifest in lack of coöperation of administrative officials in the same locality with each other, in lack of coöperation among the independent detecting and in-vestigating agencies in the same locality, in frequent lack of coöperation between local prosecutors and local courts, in friction between local courts and local administrative officials, and in lack of coöperation of court with court or even of judge with judge in the same court. Going up in the scale there has been and too often still is a like want of coöperation of locality and state. Refusal of local prosecutors, local sheriffs, and local magistrates to enforce state laws in the locality has often led to legislation providing for removal by or at the instance of some central authority. Disinclination or refusal of local police to enforce state laws have often led to the setting up of state commissions to appoint and control municipal police. State police have been called for to give effect to state regulations as against local obstruction, and the old spirit reappears now and then in conflicts between state police and local constables and local police.

Again, want of coöperation as between different bureaus or services, even when under the same department, in the Federal Government was conspicuous in the attempt to enforce prohibition, and noncoöperation of the administrative officials and the prosecuting agencies and the Federal courts was an everyday matter.

A want of coöperation of state with state, in a confederation in which there was no adequate provision for a central government was one of the chief occasions of our Federal constitution. But the powers of our central government are limited, and in many matters which have ceased to be local, the old attitude of noncoöperation and indifference to the general, as contrasted with the local, security remains. This attitude has been even more marked in the matter of coöperation of state and Federal agencies. State interference with enforcement of Federal laws, Federal interference with state enforcement of state laws, conflicts of jurisdiction between Federal and state courts with respect to the same property or controversy, and indifference of Federal and state governments to enforcement of each other's laws have written some strange things in our law reports. In the present generation there has been a good beginning in the direction of conscious systematic coöperation between national and state authorities. That there is a growing spirit of coöperation is manifest. But it is significant that this spirit did not begin to grow until our polity was a century old. No less significant is the value now put upon coöperation where in the last century the value put on free individual self-assertion was so high that what seem to us absurdities did not seem too great a price to pay for the extreme official and local independence.

Nor has this indifference to coöperation been confined to agencies of government and administration. An idea of coöperation is much closer to the realities of industry than the conventional idea of free individual self-assertion. After all, employer and employees are coöperating in great enterprises. It is wasteful to regard them, and so lead them to regard themselves, as necessarily and at all events engaged in contests with each other.

Moreover, this idea of coöperation is much nearer to the realities of urban life today than the idea of competitive free self-assertion by which we go on measuring. Simply ask yourself, as to your own city, how many are freely competing, and how many more are doing their part, perhaps in a modest way, as employees in some great corporate enterprise, finding a reflected glory in its greatness and giving it service in return for protection in a relation very like the old one of lord and man?

If coöperation is not to be the whole idea, it is to be a large part of it. But I prefer to think that the recognition of coöperation and new emphasis upon it in all connections is a step toward some ideal involving organized human effort along with free spontaneous individual initiative, and I seem to see such an ideal in the idea of civilization. Indeed, there are signs that twentieth-century law, in the sense both of the body of authoritative materials of decision and of the judicial process, as well as twentieth-century juristic thinking, along with concern for the concrete individual life instead of the abstract individual will, are concerned for civilization as distinct from and contrasted with politically organized society. Since the Reformation, politically organized society has asserted a paramountcy, and largely maintained it, which has sometimes made it appear an end rather than a means. But the most extreme advocates of an omnicompetent state have not ventured to go so far.

An ideal of civilization, of raising human powers to their highest possible unfolding, of the maximum of human control over external nature and over internal nature for human purposes, must recognize two factors in achieving that control: on the one hand, free individual initiative, spontaneous self-assertion of individual men; and on the other hand, coöperative, ordered, if you will, regimented activity. Neither can be ignored if we are to maintain, go forward with, and hand down control over nature. Not the least achievement of recent thought has been to rid us of the idea of the *unum necessarium*. We are no longer bound to believe that only one of the two, individual freedom of action and coöperative organized activity, can be taken account of in our picture of human life. We are not precluded from an ideal which allows both for competition and for coöperation. We are not compelled, because we recognize coöperation as a factor in civilization, to sacrifice all that was achieved in the last century by working out a system of individual rights, or what has been achieved through and since the Puritan revolution toward securing individual freedom as a no less essential factor.

It will have been seen that of the three methods of valuing interests open to law-makers and courts and jurists, the third, which has been the main reliance of the jurist, and the second, much urged in the present century, are now less useful, indeed are embarrassed in their operation, because of transition from a social order for which the received ideal had been shaped and the jural postulates of which were clearly under-stood, to one which has not sufficiently found itself to admit of formulating an ideal which all will accept (as all the schools accepted that of the last century) or formu-lating jural postulates of the validity of which we may be assured. Yet the practical work of the courts in adjusting relations and ordering conduct must go on. The legal order cannot stand still until philosophers can agree, as they did in the last century, on an ideal, and the legal profession and the courts can be induced or educated to receive it as authoritative. It cannot stand still until the social order has settled down for a time in a condition of stability in which its jural postulates can be recognized and formulated and the principles derived from them can be received into the authoritative guides to determination of controversies. In the meantime the courts must, as in the past, go on finding out by experience and developing by reason the modes of adjusting relations and ordering conduct which will give the most effect to the whole scheme of interests with the least friction and the least waste.

INDEX